Samuel French Acting Edition

Yoga Play

by Dipika Guha

SAMUEL FRENCH

ISBN 978-0-573-70852-7

www.concordtheatricals.com
www.concordtheatricals.co.uk

FOR PRODUCTION ENQUIRIES

UNITED STATES AND CANADA
info@concordtheatricals.com
1-866-979-0447

UNITED KINGDOM AND EUROPE
licensing@concordtheatricals.co.uk
020-7054-7200

Each title is subject to availability from Concord Theatricals, depending upon country of performance. Please be aware that *YOGA PLAY* may not be licensed by Concord Theatricals in your territory. Professional and amateur producers should contact the nearest Concord Theatricals office or licensing partner to verify availability.

This work is published by Samuel French, an imprint of Concord Theatricals.

YOGA PLAY was commissioned and first produced by South Coast Repertory, with support from the Time Warner Foundation, in Costa Mesa, California on April 21, 2017. The performance was directed by Crispin Whittell, with sets by Se Hyun Oh, costumes by Kathryn Poppen, lighting by Adam J. Frank, sound by Crick S. Myers, and projections by Lianne Arnold. The production stage manager was Bradley Zipser. The cast was as follows:

JOAN .... Nike Doukas
RAJ .... Dileep Rao
FRED .... Tim Chiou
ROMOLA / ENSEMBLE .... Lorena Martinez
BERNARD BROWN / ENSEMBLE .... Jeff Marlow

CHARACTERS

JOHN DALE – Founder of Jojomon, fifties, like an aging rock star

JOAN – early fifties, white, American

RAJ – mid-thirties, South-Asian, American

FRED – mid-thirties, Singaporean

ROMOLA – mid-twenties, Latina, American

GURUJI* – early forties/fifties

MR. KAPOOR* – Raj's father, early sixties, shouty, upper-class North Indian accent

ALAN CARR* – BBC News reporter, a bit nasal, classic BBC cadence

MRS. KAPOOR** – Raj's mother, early sixties, heavy upper-class North Indian accent

LUCY** – Jojomon employee, mid-twenties, highly-educated, American

NOOYI** – Joan's secretary, early/mid-twenties, over-keen, American

LAUREN LILLY CLARK ROSE** – Jojomon brand ambassador, American

*played by the actor playing **JOHN DALE**

played by the actor playing **ROMOLA

SETTING

Jojomon HQ, Southern California.

A high-end yoga studio, Southern California.

And the internet.

TIME

The present.

AUTHOR'S NOTES

Doubling

The actor playing John Dale also plays Alan Carr, Mr. Kapoor, and Guruji. The actor playing Romola also plays Lucy, Nooyi, Mrs. Kapoor, and Lauren Lilly Clark Rose.

Punctuation

A slash (/) signals overlapping dialogue.
(Text in parentheses) is spoken aloud as an aside, or alternatively as a comment made *sotto voce*.

Production

There are some moments where the actor playing Lucy or Lauren Lilly Clark Rose overlaps with Nooyi. Since all these parts are played by the same actor, in production, you may cut the moments of overlap – or make the choice to pre-record Nooyi's voice.

ACT I

1.

(Jojomon HQ.)

*(***JOAN***,* ***RAJ****, and* ***FRED*** *sit around a conference table, reading from documents. Behind them on Skype is company founder and Jojomon legend,* ***JOHN DALE****. He's snacking.)*

JOAN. Jojomon is up 16.85% from 12% in the last fiscal year. Top-line growth's expected to come in between 9 and 13%, with revenues in the range of 1.97 to 2.02 billion dollars. Revenue gains will be spurred by same-store sales growth in the mid-single digits as well as e-commerce sales, which we anticipate will be higher.

*(***JOHN*** *takes a big swig from a Jojomon water bottle.)*

...Our stock's price-to-earnings multiple is at thirty-three, eleven points higher than that of the S&P 500 index.

*(***JOHN*** *spills on his shirt and ducks out of sight.)*

Operating income rate has shrunk 540 basis points to 14.2%, while both excess inventory and operating expenses have risen. So as you probably can tell, I have some thoughts about that.

John? Are you there?

JOHN. *(Popping back up.)* Yeah, sorry... I just spilled something down my...sorry...

I'm here.

JOAN. I'd like to place our attention on yoga apparel development, marketing, and supply chain investments. R&D has been working very hard and I'm excited by what / we've come up with.

JOHN. Can I just...can I just interject here Joan?

JOAN. By all means.

(**JOHN** *inhales deeply.*)

JOHN. I can just feel already Joan, that we, the company, this...precious family are safe in your hands. Not that we weren't with Brad. You know, as men, our intention is never to disparage women, so when Brad said quote "that it was the size of women's thighs that were making the Kayala fabric transparent not the fabric itself," what he was talking about was something...much more circumstantial than essential, you know?

(No one knows what that means.)

...I just, I'm sorry, Brad, Brad and I were very close, and you know, I'm still adjusting...

(**JOAN** *looks at* **RAJ** *and* **FRED**, *who indicate that she should keep going.*)

JOAN. I understand John. Shall I continue?

JOHN. Oh yeah yeah – of course.

JOAN. Before I share this with the company / I wanted –

JOHN. The family.

JOAN. The...family. I want to share with you the vision that we...

JOHN. SIT.

(**JOAN** *looks baffled.*)

STAY. Down. No... DOWN.

(**JOAN** *looks offended.*)

There's a goo gurl...there's a goo girl...

(A yippy bark in the background.)

RAJ. Is uh Sappho with you John?

JOHN. Oh she just goes everywhere with me don't ya Sapph... she luuuves the beach, she just, sorry she's just so cute when she puts her paws out like that, like a judge!

FRED. John hi, it's Fred. Joan is just talking about our new idea.

JOHN. Right... Joan! Please. Go ahead.

JOAN. I'll be brief. I'm very proud to present to you our new concept fabric, Joyon.

Inspired by best-selling author Marie Kondo's "if it sparks joy" motif, Joyon follows the very same, very simple premise; our clothes, no matter who you are, where you're from or what *size* you are, will from the moment you touch them, spark *joy*.

Joyon is a powder-keg mix of premium cotton, Lycra, and nylon. When the participants of a control group experiment we ran were asked which item of clothing most sparked joy, every single one chose Joyon. The slow-release organic lavender activated by water made our participants want to hold on to their clothes even after a sweaty yoga class led by our very own brilliant brand ambassador Lauren Lilly Clark Rose.

JOHN. Lauren yay!

I love Lauren! Wasn't she out in – in...

FRED. Boulder.

JOHN. I think I took a class with her in...

FRED. Boulder

JOHN. ...Boulder I think...

FRED. The Rockies.

JOHN. Up in the Rockies I think. What was it called Fred?

FRED. Inana?

JOHN. No...

RAJ. Let me look it up...

*(**RAJ** and **FRED** both get out their cell phones and scroll madly.)*

FRED.	**RAJ.**
Shambhala Rain.	Shambhala Rain.

JOHN. That's it. Lauren had just got back from a month with Iyengar...

FRED. *(To* **JOAN.***)* (Founder of Iyengar yoga.)

JOHN. ...All he did was talk about pranayama...the mystery of the breath... *(Sadly.)* Little did we know that his was about to cease...

JOAN. We've shipped the samples to Bangladesh and after several in-depth talks with them, feel we'd like to offer Lotus Ltd the contract.

JOHN. Who?

JOAN. Lotus Ltd.

FRED. *(Helpfully.)* They're in Dhaka.

JOHN. Never heard of them.

JOAN. Turnaround is quite impressive. California could be stocked in three weeks, Hong Kong two, London four.

JOHN. Uh-huh...

JOAN. But I want to stay true to the grassroots marketing that has been so fundamental to our success and that Brad –

JOHN. Oh Brad...

JOAN. ...Was instrumental in implementing. We'll do a secret launch in three weeks through local reps in our communities where our brand ambassadors will model Joyon in favored local yoga studios. We're having them do an intense social media blitz before we launch officially on the East Coast and overseas.

JOHN. Retail?

JOAN. 200 for the yoga pants.

90 for t-shirts.

80 for underclothing.

250 for mats, / 50 for water bottles and –

JOHN. It's high Joan...

JOAN. Yes it's high but our customers / know that –

JOHN. I don't know...it's high –

JOAN. You have to see it within the context of our industry. As a country, we spent ninety-seven billion dollars on athleisure last year. Jeans sales were down, as you well know, for the first time in a decade. We're the only industry experiencing this kind of growth and frankly it's because of your good work – and of course Brad's –

(An audible sigh.)

Listen, this whole issue with Brad...

JOHN. Hurts my heart.

JOAN. I have a solution. I want us to carry size twelve.

(A strange, strangled noise involuntarily escapes **JOHN.***)*

It is important to me that all women feel included. So long as our sizes stop at eight, we are excluding a vital potential customer / base.

JOHN.	**RAJ.**	**FRED.**
Family.	Family.	Family.

JOAN. Family...base.

JOHN. How can I say this... Help me here Fred.

FRED. Oh no I agree with Joan.

RAJ. Me too.

John, I think our brand is robust enough to stretch, as it were, in this direction.

JOHN. It's not that I...agree with Brad, Joan... But just think...

Actually let's just...let's breathe together...

In...

*(***JOAN** *looks at* **RAJ** *for help, but both* **RAJ** *and* **FRED** *have closed their eyes; they instinctively reach their hands for her.)*

Out...

In...

*(***JOAN** *looks deeply uncomfortable.)*

When you hear me ring a soft bell I want you to imagine yourself as a young child...then put this child in your heart, hold her tenderly...

(The sound of a soft bell.)

JOHN. ...Now give her a little snuggle...there it is. Are we all feeling better?

RAJ. Yeah...

FRED. *(Clearing his throat.)* Totally (sorry, cleaned out some phlegm.)

*(**JOHN** chuckles knowingly.)*

JOHN. I know what's happening here. After all the damage we men have done, it's time that men got out of the way, I see that. But our brand Joan, is *aspirational.* I just want us to consider the kind of message we're sending if we were to run in plus sizes I just / think that –

*(**JOAN** hits the mute button momentarily. **JOHN** doesn't know and continues to talk animatedly.)*

JOAN. (Size twelve is not plus-size – someone tell him.)

RAJ. Nope.

FRED. Unwise.

*(**JOAN** unmutes **JOHN**.)*

JOHN. ...Alienate the core members of our family who have been with us / from day one.

JOAN. I hear you John, I really do. But it is difficult to stand by the idea that these products create joy if you can't get them on.

JOHN. What are the projections?

JOAN. 68 million –

JOHN. Well –

JOAN. In the first quarter.

(A stunned moment.)

JOHN. *(Fully reversing.)* Ultimately all of this is about creating deep happiness, creating value in people's lives.

You're a talented gal Joan. Your TED Talk on female leadership was beyond educational!

JOAN. Thank you.

JOHN. Are you feeling better Joan?

(A moment.)

JOAN. It means a lot to me to be here...to be working again. And you know, I'm...I'm very grateful to you John.

JOHN. Let me tell you this, the real reason for our success...

FRED. (Marketing.)

JOHN. Authenticity.

FRED. (Right, authenticity.)

JOAN. I couldn't agree more. And now I think we should expand this mission to include women in a variety of sizes.

JOHN. ...

Yes. All right. Okay.

JOAN. Okay?

JOHN. Yes. Okay.

JOAN. That's wonderful!

JOHN. Who's out there in Bangladesh?

RAJ. Lucy and Neil arrived in Dhaka two days ago.

JOHN. They having fun?

FRED. As far as we can tell. Notwithstanding heat and culture shock.

JOHN. Isn't Neil Bangladeshi?

RAJ. In the same way I'm Punjabi.

From Delaware.

JOHN. You're both from Delaware? What are the chances!

He's so skinny. His immune system looks so compromised to me. I tried to get him to play golf. How's the old backswing Raj?

RAJ. Good good, Fred and I are getting out to Oak Creek this weekend.

JOHN. Gosh that sounds like fun. How's your mother Fred? Is she well?

FRED. Better John – and even better now I'm sending more money home ha ha!

JOHN. How's your practice Joan?

JOAN. Oh. It's – it's going well

JOHN. Uh-huh. It can be challenging I know. Joan, when I get back, we're going to have to do some serious vinyasa together. Really get into rhythm.

JOAN. Uhm-hm. That sounds...wonderful. Can't wait.

JOHN. Meanwhile, I'm tuning off. Four weeks, no phone, no internet, no nothing. I'm leaving it all in your capable hands.

NO LICKING SAPPHO.

THAT'S RUDE.

(A click.)

*(**JOAN** looks a bit rattled.)*

RAJ. All right!

FRED. Bring on the celebration smoothies!

JOAN. I still don't know / when you're kidding.

RAJ. He's kidding.

FRED. I'm kidding. Congratulations team!

RAJ. Masterful, Joan.

FRED. Big shoes to fill and I have to say, you're filling them so nicely.

JOAN. Raj, call Lucy about Bangladesh...

RAJ. Right, yes.

(He goes to leave.)

JOAN. Actually, no, no – wait.

RAJ. What?

JOAN. Is there something we're...

I feel like there's something I've overlooked.

*(**FRED** hands his iPad to **JOAN**.)*

FRED. Well, here's my list.

Brand management has the latest.

Ad campaign's approved.

JOAN. We have all the information from the focus groups?

RAJ. Yeah we've got all that.

*(**JOAN**'s breathing starts to shorten.)*

JOAN. I just – I don't know...
I guess the first month in any job's always crazy huh?

*(**FRED** checks his watch.)*

RAJ. You want to go home and practice?

JOAN. Uh...no. I think I just...maybe, no, no, yes.
Call Lucy.

FRED. Are you okay?

JOAN. I just need some fresh air.

*(**RAJ** and **FRED** go to leave.)*

RAJ. Hey, Joan – congratulations.
We're lucky to have you.

2.

*(**RAJ** and **FRED** eat their lunch. It's green juice. They look hungry.)*

RAJ. I sometimes dream of them.

FRED. Babies?

RAJ. Yeah, babies.
I dream I'm giving birth to them.

FRED. Through your penis?

RAJ. Yeah...they pop out of there.
I had a dream last night that I'm on a plane and my stomach was stretched out to here and the flight is long and I'm nervous that we'd run out of time and I'd give birth right here.

FRED. Oh my god –

RAJ. And then when we arrive at the airport, my stomach is flat and I'm like "oh my god – I must've miscarried" and then suddenly I see a head peeking out of my body –

FRED. Ew – / that's disgusting lah!

RAJ. Yeah – yeah! And then I give birth to this thing and it is covered in a kind of flaky chicken skin.

FRED. Jesus. Do you think it's because things are...

RAJ. Changing around here? Yes, yes I do.

FRED. Joan's awesome but she's –

RAJ. Moving like the wind...

FRED. It's making my head spin –

RAJ. My stomach's been a little iffy.

FRED. What? You'll have to get that checked out.

RAJ. Really?

FRED. Yeah, you don't want it to get out that you're –

(Scans over his shoulder, then whispers:)

(Stressed.)

RAJ. I'm not (stressed.)

FRED. You look (stressed.)

(He gets up to leave.)

RAJ. Where are you going? It's dreamtime.

FRED. I thought we finished dreamtime.

RAJ. Now we have to process dreamtime –

FRED. I'm going to the gym –

RAJ. Do you have to go now?

FRED. If I don't go now (no one will see me go…)

RAJ. What the hell are you doing *Fred*?

FRED. I'm being a good employee *Raj*…
Why aren't you at yoga?

RAJ. I no longer do yoga.

FRED. What??? Why?

RAJ. It's (*stressful.*)

FRED. What's wrong with you?

RAJ. I just – I don't know.
Goal Tuesday's coming up.

FRED. Wasn't your goal "run a marathon"?

RAJ. Yeah.

FRED. Didn't you do that?

RAJ. Yeah.

FRED. Then what's the…

RAJ. That's not my real goal.

FRED. You wrote down fake goals?

RAJ. I'm not giving up my real goals, man. That's private.

FRED. Here at Jojomon "when we share our goals we improve ourselves."

RAJ. Speak for yourself.

FRED. How are you going to improve yourself in private?

RAJ. Maybe I don't need improving.

FRED. That why you're single?

RAJ. I'm picky.
How's your mother?

FRED. You try to make that an insult.

Well I don't hear an insult, I hear a question.
She's fine.
My mother put me through college –

RAJ. Okay, okay, let's not get / into this.

FRED. She took out loans!
Did your mother take out loans for Harvard?

RAJ. No. I got a ride.

FRED. Harvard Business School doesn't give free rides.

RAJ. ...From my parents.

FRED. I hate you.
What's your goal? I'll tell you mine.

RAJ. Your visa's gonna get renewed Fred.

FRED. Shhhhhh...
What's your goal?

RAJ. I just –

FRED. What'syourgoal?

RAJ. I just want to –

FRED. What'syourgoalwhat'syourgoalwhat'syourgoal?

RAJ. I want to feel...?

FRED. ...
You're joking?

RAJ. Forget it.

FRED. Seriously?

RAJ. Doesn't matter.

FRED. I have to pay my niece's school fees and buy my mother a fridge and you want to feel "..."

RAJ. Drink your lunch.

3.

*(**JOAN** sits at her desk. Skype call dial-up sound. We hear the first few beats. **LUCY** appears onscreen; her image is a bit blurry. The light is white behind her.)*

JOAN. Well, you've heard?

LUCY. Yeah I heard! I saw on CNN.

JOAN. You're blurry Lucy I'm turning you off.

*(**LUCY** disappears.)*

Shit. Are you still there?

LUCY. Yeah, I'm here. It's *great*! They're flying off the shelves!

JOAN. And you know if we can sell size twelve...

LUCY. We can sell fourteen?

JOAN. Exactly.

LUCY. A coup for your comeback!

JOAN. What do you mean comeback?

LUCY. Huh?

JOAN. It was a sabbatical.

LUCY. Of course it was...

That's...exactly what we heard.

JOAN. What exactly did you hear?

LUCY. *(Uh-oh.)* ...

Hm?

JOAN. ...I wasn't gone that long...

LUCY. Oh, yeah, no yeah, no – of course.

Uhm, how are the guys?

JOAN. *(Moving on.)* Good, I think. Bit...weird. How are things in Dhaka?

LUCY. They're good. Oh wait – ciao Mina! – my cook's leaving.

JOAN. Cook! Lovely.

LUCY. I don't know. It's a little weird. But I'm getting used to someone making me lunch every day. I have a little tiffin box.

JOAN. A little what?

LUCY. A little...

JOAN. Like a lunch box?

LUCY. Yeah – but like stainless steel. And round and they stack up.

JOAN. I've seen those.

(Her intercom buzzes.)

Stay there Lucy.

(To intercom.) What is it Nooyi?

NOOYI. *(Through intercom.)* Fred's here to see you.

JOAN. I'm on a call Nooyi.

FRED. *(Through intercom.)* (Tell her it's urgent.)

NOOYI. *(Through intercom.)* He says it's urgent.

JOAN. Lucy I'm sorry, / she knows I'm on a call.

LUCY. That's okay!

*(**FRED** enters. **JOAN**'s intercom buzzes.)*

JOAN. *(To intercom.)* What is it Nooyi?

NOOYI. *(Through intercom.)* He's inside.

JOAN. *(To intercom.)* Yes, I know I can see him.

FRED. I have to / speak to you.

NOOYI. *(Through intercom.)* Joan can I –

FRED. It's important

JOAN. *(To intercom.)* Not now Nooyi.

*(She hangs up on **NOOYI**.)*

What is it Fred?

*(To **LUCY** on Skype.)* Lucy – I'll call you back –

FRED. No, no – wait.

*(He rushes to **JOAN**'s desk.)*

Lucy. Hi it's Fred.

LUCY. Hi Fred!

FRED. Have you heard of Alan Carr?

LUCY. No...who's that?

FRED. He's out in Dhaka with you.

LUCY. Oh – is he / from sales?

FRED. No he's part of a BBC investigative team.

JOAN.	**LUCY.**
What?	What?

FRED. Have you been to the Lotus Factory Lucy?

LUCY. Yeah – a couple of times.

FRED. Everything look okay to you?

LUCY. Yes, it did / I mean.

FRED. Well, Alan Carr was there last week and he's going to prove that over three-fourths of the women you met are really children.

(He hands **JOAN** *a manila folder.)*

Lucy?

LUCY. I'm here. I'm confused.

FRED. He has proof that a lot of those women are twelve. Did they look twelve to you?
Lucy???

LUCY. I mean, everyone here is quite small...and they cover their heads / a lot of them...

JOAN. When does it air?

FRED. Tonight.

(The sound of the Twitterverse explodes.)

LUCY. Oh my god. Joan it's on Twitter.

FRED. Oh my god – it's on the news, it's on Twitter.

LUCY. Hashtag –

LUCY.	**FRED.**
Evilmonyoga!	Evilmonyoga!
What's happening?	
Joan?	
Joan??	Joan??!

4.

*(***RAJ, JOAN,*** and ***FRED.*** Joan's office. Projected behind them, BBC correspondent ***ALAN CARR*** stands in front of a crumbling factory over music in the style of* Panorama.[*]*)*

ALAN CARR. *(Standard BBC reporter, slightly nasal.)* When Bangladeshi garment factory Rana Plaza collapsed, an industry promised to change. But over the last five weeks *Panorama*'s secret investigation has found workers locked inside factories forced to work incredibly long shifts and most alarmingly, children as young as nine working twelve-hour days to feed their families. We started our investigation at the Lotus factory in Dhaka where we discovered sixty percent of the workers were underage girls slaving over designs for fashion brand Jojomon, whose yoga apparel famously retail for hundreds of / dollars –

*(***JOAN*** presses stop.)*

JOAN. What do you have?

FRED. Fifteen thousand emails.

RAJ. A hundred thousand tweets.

JOAN. That's not so bad.

FRED. And a couple of death threats.
Oh and Alan Carr wants a statement.

JOAN. They have our statement.

FRED. They want a better statement.

RAJ. What happened?

FRED. Lotus was subcontracting to a conglomerate of factories outside of Dhaka.

RAJ. So it was a front.

---

*A license to produce *Yoga Play* does not include a performance license for any third-party or copyrighted music. Licensees should create an original composition or use music in the public domain. For further information, please see Music Use Note on page 3.

FRED. A squeaky-clean front.

RAJ. And the others?

FRED. Mob-owned. Overrun by rats, open sewers, rampant typhoid.

JOAN. Where's Cassie?

FRED. They're working on the redraft.

JOAN. Did you think we didn't sound sorry enough?

RAJ. I thought we sounded very sorry.

JOAN. Then what was the problem?

FRED. We need something else.

A lot of the backlash has come from the family.

JOAN. *Your* family?

FRED. The customers! They feel betrayed, let down, manipulated –

RAJ. They truly believe they're our family so they're reacting like a family member turned on them. They're angry.

JOAN. *(Thinking.)* They're saying they're angry.

But what they're feeling...is guilty.

*(**RAJ** and **FRED** take this in.)*

Fred, get Lauren what'shername to do a live-streaming session on self-healing. Get the rest of the brand ambassadors to focus on self-forgiveness and letting go. And Raj, you have our yoga studio partners schedule free yoga classes!

FRED. We can't just ask them to give / them away.

JOAN. Then buy them.

RAJ. Wait, what was the social media takeaway again?

FRED. We're accused of being fake.

RAJ. Why fake?

FRED. We sent it all over to our big data people who analyzed the feedback and that's the word that's coming up over and over again. Fake, inauthentic, / pseudo–

RAJ. We didn't know that they were subcontracting – people should / know that.

JOAN. This is not about Bangladesh. This is about regaining trust with our customers.

FRED.	**RAJ.**
Family!	Family!

FRED. We could...distract them!

RAJ. With what? A sale?

FRED. We don't *do* sales Raj.

RAJ. I know *Fred.*

FRED. We could do something proactive! We weren't the only ones on this list –

RAJ. We're the only ones who don't advertise.

FRED. We could contact GAP, Abercrombie and Walmart. Rally some sort of ethical pressure group –

RAJ. They're the perpetrators, we can't be seen mingling with the perps!

JOAN. Shhhhh.

Just let me think.

For a moment.

(A moment.)

How does the family feel about John?

RAJ. Uh –

FRED. They love him.

RAJ. ...But since the whole Brad thing...

FRED. They've been understanding.

RAJ. ...And the mid-life crisis slash dating models thing –

FRED. Why?

JOAN. We have data that proves that the closer the company's culture is to its founder's vision, the greater the loyalty the custo– family has to the product. John said it himself, the real reason for our success is –

FRED. (Marketing.)

JOAN. Authenticity.

FRED. (Right, authenticity!)

RAJ. So what you're saying is...

JOAN. We are not having an *ethical* crisis.

RAJ. No??

JOAN. No.

FRED. No?

So what is it that we are having?

JOAN. We are having...an *authenticity* crisis. So, what we need to do is to find some way to re-establish our *authenticity* in the marketplace.

FRED. How?

JOAN. As per the data, we need to emphasize Jojomon's relationship to...

RAJ. John?

JOAN. ...No not John, that's not going to work! Is there no one else who has the same kind of authority?

RAJ. Uh well, John studied with someone who studied with, who was that Fred?

(**FRED** *scrolls through his phone.*)

FRED. Yogi Bhajan?

RAJ. *(Mispronouncing.)* No not Yogi Bhayjan – before Yogi Bhayjan. Vivekaynanda?

FRED. *(Pronouncing correctly.)* Vivekananda.

RAJ. Yogurtnanda?

FRED. *(Pronouncing correctly.)* Yogananda.

Those guys are dead.

RAJ. So, no.

(A moment.)

JOAN. When John goes offline...does he go completely offline?

RAJ. Oh yeah – when he's off he's / off –

FRED. We don't hear from him for weeks.

JOAN. Good. So we have a little time.

RAJ. For / what?

JOAN. What if we found someone.

With that same kind of authority.

FRED. Like a...like?

JOAN. ...Someone with real, you know, credentials –
Who could appeal...for us...

FRED. You mean –

JOAN. Find me a guru.

FRED. From where?

JOAN. Start with the obvious.
LA.

5.

(**JOAN** *and* **ROMOLA**. *A high-end yoga studio.* **ROMOLA** *is doing a terribly difficult yoga pose with great ease.)*

(Meditative music.)*

ROMOLA. Namaste.

JOAN. Hi...

ROMOLA. You must be Joan!

JOAN. Yes, that's me.

ROMOLA. You're Jane's friend? I looooove Jane. My mom would go to work and leave me with her exercise videos and now we're doing downward dogs together so – Dreams do come true.

JOAN. I don't know Jane Fonda.

ROMOLA. No?

JOAN. No.

ROMOLA. Oh – I'm sorry – I thought she recommended you...we normally don't give / appointments to –

JOAN. I pulled some strings. Which I would not have done but this is kind of an emergency.

ROMOLA. A yoga emergency?

JOAN. Yes.

ROMOLA. Mmm yes...because your aura is very grey?

JOAN. No... I mean, maybe, but no.

ROMOLA. Because your spirit is fading?

JOAN. No!

ROMOLA. Because if you don't reconnect to your heart chakra, you'll die?

(**JOAN**'s *breath starts to shorten.)*

---

*A license to produce *Yoga Play* does not include a performance license for any third-party or copyrighted music. Licensees should create an original composition or use music in the public domain. For further information, please see Music Use Note on page 3.

JOAN. Look here...

ROMOLA. Romola...

But my real name is Patanjali Shri.

Given to me by our founder Clare Swami Smith –

(**JOAN** *recovers.*)

JOAN. Oh is she the head teacher?

ROMOLA. No Clare no longer practices yoga.

JOAN. What does she do?

ROMOLA. She makes cheese.

JOAN. I see.

ROMOLA. She's following her bliss.

JOAN. You look awfully young –

ROMOLA. Thank you! Twenty-five is the new nineteen that's what they say!

JOAN. (Oh my god.)

ROMOLA. Did you say something?

JOAN. Romona –

ROMOLA. Romola –

JOAN. Yes, my sources tell me that you are LA's best yoga place.

ROMOLA. We're LA's premier Yoga, Spa and Wellness Institute, / yes.

JOAN. Right – excellent.

So if I needed to find a teacher.

I mean, a real teacher.

ROMOLA. You're in the right place.

We have aerial yoga, prenatal yoga, Pilates yoga, heated power yoga, weight training yoga, goat yoga...

JOAN. Do you have...authentic yoga?

ROMOLA. Well, each teacher teaches differently depending / on what you want to get out of it.

JOAN. I mean, original yoga. Pure yoga.

Do you know what I'm talking about?

ROMOLA. Not really.

JOAN. Me neither.

ROMOLA. Do you mean traditional yoga?

JOAN. Yes that's what I mean!

(She checks her phone.)

Look. I'm in a bit of a rush. This is kind of an emergency.

ROMOLA. You said. There are a lot of places that do traditional yoga – and a lot of good teachers.

JOAN. But I thought that / you were –

ROMOLA. Well, I can make you look really good.

And feel really good – but I'm not sure / that that's what you're here for.

JOAN. Just a sec –

(She makes a phone call.)

She's useless.

We're going to have to look further afield.

Get me everyone from the last fifty years.

They're yogis, they live long right?

(She hangs up.)

Okay.

Thank you.

(She leaves.)

ROMOLA. We didn't close out with intention! This is a four-hundred-dollar session and you could use it! NAMASTE!!! Namaste.

6.

*(**JOAN**, **RAJ**, and **FRED**. Conference room. They stare in a long silence at a PowerPoint presentation that has one word on it: GURU. **RAJ** hits his clicker.)*

RAJ. Guru: "Sanskrit term connoting someone who is a 'teacher, guide, expert, or master' who helps one to discover the same potentialities that the guru has already realized. The syllable Gu means darkness, the syllable Ru, he who dispels it." And as far as I can tell, a guru or yogi is someone who has given up their worldly life and takes off, sometimes shoeless, into the uh... wilderness.

JOAN. You mean they've renounced?

RAJ. Yes, a yogi is someone who's renounced the world.

JOAN. No Raj, a yogi is a young woman with a yoga mat and a lavender latte.

RAJ. Right, yes, yes, / yes sorry –

JOAN. We need someone who can bring in the old wisdom and fit smoothly into our brand image.

FRED. So what exactly are we looking for?

JOAN. Someone who can reassure the...family that we at Jojomon are closer than ever to the message at the core of our...our –

FRED. Billion-dollar company?

JOAN. Vision!

FRED. (Right, vision!)

JOAN. Someone with charisma and power who can re-establish our authenticity through his or her presence without harming the core brand language that has worked so well for us.

FRED. So, I don't know if we have that exactly, but Raj and I made a list.

*(He hands **JOAN** his iPad.)*

JOAN. Where are they?

FRED. India. Living ones on the left, dead ones on the right –

JOAN. Why would I want a dead guru?

RAJ. They seem like they're what we'd want...

JOAN. But – they're dead.

FRED. Right...but we wanted to leave room for...

RAJ. Uhm...you say it.

FRED. No it's your religion you say it!

RAJ. ...Reincarnation?

*(**JOAN** stares at **RAJ**.)*

(A long moment.)

JOAN. And you have data on this?

RAJ. No...

JOAN. Then we don't have the time, but thank you for considering it.

FRED.	**RAJ.**
You're welcome.	Totally.

JOAN. Talk me through these.

RAJ. Okay – so let's begin with Anjali Poori.

(He taps through his PowerPoint presentation, which shows the respective gurus' stats accompanied by a photograph where their faces are somewhat unhelpfully obscured.)

JOAN. A woman, that's good.

RAJ. She has her own university, they do disaster relief, public health, building homes, / female empowerment –

JOAN. Excellent –

RAJ. But –

JOAN. But what?

RAJ. She's old.

JOAN. How old?

RAJ.	**FRED.**
A hundred.	A hundred.

JOAN. Too old.

FRED. I don't see sexy on the memo.
Do we want sexy?

JOAN. Wouldn't hurt.

FRED. Facial hair?
I mean, not for women, / obviously.

RAJ. Facial hair polled highly in our focus group surveys –

FRED. That's because they're all hipsters.

JOAN. That's our demographic Fred.

FRED. And believe me, I'm grateful.

JOAN. Who else? Who else?

RAJ. Pandit Jyoti Das. Just recently he brokered the peace deal between the Colombian government and FARC.

JOAN. FARC? We can't have Joyon associated with guerilla warfare.

FRED. Baba Sitaram. He has his own company Moksha Bliss.

RAJ. They make organic plant-based products.

FRED. Manufacturing is out of Dehradun north of Delhi.

JOAN. How did he raise his capital?

FRED. Private equity.

JOAN. Really?

RAJ. Last year they made 670 million.

JOAN. Rupees?

RAJ. Dollars.

JOAN. Jesus. We need him on our board.

(A moment.)

I don't know...

FRED. What?

JOAN. These people don't sound very...

FRED. What?

JOAN. Spiritual.

RAJ. But...that's all that they do.

JOAN. But, going by your definition, what exactly have they renounced?

RAJ. Well, I think they're celibate.

JOAN. So am I! It doesn't make me – sorry / I didn't mean to –

RAJ.	**FRED.**
No worries!	Ancient history!

JOAN. Look at this website – it's nicer than ours, I'm concerned that their brand presence might actually outstrip ours.

RAJ. So...

What you're saying is we need a less Main Street guru...

And more an off-off-the-beaten-path guru...

JOAN. I thought being a guru *was* kind of off-off the beaten path.

FRED. On the contrary, it's a very lucrative career option in an under-saturated global market.

RAJ. But if we want someone who's not online, who's truly out there we'd –

FRED. What?

RAJ. We'd have to go.

FRED. To India?

RAJ. Yeah.

FRED. Can't Lucy –

JOAN. Lucy doesn't work for us anymore.

*(**FRED** and **RAJ** stare at **JOAN**, perhaps for the first time realizing their jobs are on the line.)*

RAJ.	**FRED.**
Shit really?	Shit...

JOAN. We're going to announce it at the company meeting tomorrow.

*(**FRED** recovers first.)*

FRED. So even if we went ourselves, got on the next flight... which looks like it's at noon, that's still sixteen hours, fifty-five minutes (scratch that there are no direct flights), that's twenty-two hours thirty minutes, we'd arrive tomorrow at noon, a day for research, a day for procurement and then in order to give Marketing –

JOAN. I want to run them through Creative first –

FRED. Why do we need Creative?

JOAN. I want them to run whatever he or she –

FRED. Or they –

JOAN. Or they?

FRED. Moving us gently away from the gender binary –

JOAN. Oh I see, yes or *they* say into our existing brand language.

FRED. But we're then counting on fresh intel to lead us to the right person all in forty-eight hours...that's going to be hard. And by hard I mean, a fucking huge gamble, excuse my English.

(Silence.)

(More silence.)

RAJ. Okay so...shit, I'm probably gonna regret this but...

JOAN. What?

RAJ. So...my parents are kind of up on all things Hindu.

FRED. You mean they are Hindu?

RAJ. Yeah – because you have to be born Hindu to be Hindu, so they are, but they're actually both atheist *but* they have that super-Indian-nostalgia because they've been here since the sixties and there's kind of a guilt and a romanticism about not going back. So they go to temples a lot, keep up with Hindu stuff you know, culturally so my mom...might just know of some gurus that her friends are / into.

JOAN. Call her.

RAJ. *(Checking his watch.)* It's kind of late on the East Coast now – so –

JOAN. Call her.

*(**RAJ** gets on his phone.)*

Put her on speaker.

RAJ. I don't know if that's –

JOAN. Raj.

RAJ. Okay.

*(As the call is answered, **RAJ** hits the speaker button.)*

MRS. KAPOOR. *(Through speaker phone, heavy upper-class Indian accent.)* Raju?

RAJ. Hi Mom.

MRS. KAPOOR. *(Belligerent.)* Where have you been?

RAJ. Working.

MRS. KAPOOR. If I had said I was "working" when you needed your bottom cleaning, / where would you be?

RAJ. Mom listen, I'm in kind of a hurry. I need you to give me the names of some gurus.

MR. KAPOOR. *(In the background.)* (WHO IS IT??)

MRS. KAPOOR. It's your son.

MR. KAPOOR. (WHICH ONE??)

MRS. KAPOOR. What do you mean which one? You only have one son!

*(**RAJ** looks nervously at **FRED** and **JOAN**. A slow smile is spreading across **FRED**'s face.)*

RAJ. Mom –

MRS. KAPOOR. Why do you need this?

RAJ. For work.

MRS. KAPOOR. How are you going to meet someone if / all you do is work?

RAJ. Mom –

MRS. KAPOOR. Raju gurus are all very well but psychotherapy might be even better, / you know, your father and I –

RAJ. Mom gurus please!

MR. KAPOOR. (WHAT DOES HE WANT?)

MRS. KAPOOR. He wants some names of gurus.

MR. KAPOOR. (JYOTI DAS.)

MRS. KAPOOR. That's actually a good idea – do you know Shri Jyoti Das? He's got that big temple in Gurgaon?

RAJ. Yep have him.

MRS. KAPOOR. You've got Jyoti? Ooh...and how about that Baba? / Who was that? Ram Shri! Baba Ram Shri.

MR. KAPOOR. (ARREY! RAM SHRI!)

RAJ. Yeah he's on our list.

(We hear **MRS. KAPOOR** *moving around with the phone.* **MR. KAPOOR** *now sounds closer.)*

MRS. KAPOOR. ...Jai, who's that guy?

RAJ. Name Mom! I need a name!

MRS. KAPOOR. Name is coming, name is coming...

MR. KAPOOR. (Baba Gopal Rao.)

MRS. KAPOOR. Baba Gopal Rao!

That's it!

He does yoga, he's very very famous.

But there was some...

RAJ. What?

MR. KAPOOR. (Raping women!)

MRS. KAPOOR. Oh yes. There was that.

RAJ. No we can't have rapists Mom! Look, never mind – / I'll just

MRS. KAPOOR. No no – wait a minute beta –

Let me think... Guru...

Not a rapist...

That's going to be difficult Raju –

MR. KAPOOR. (Very difficult.)

MRS. KAPOOR. Actually...there is someone.

Your Chacha went up to see him quite recently, no Jai?

*(***JOAN** *and* **FRED** *perk up.* **FRED** *grabs his iPad.)*

RAJ. Is it an ashram?

MRS. KAPOOR. I think it might be...in the Himalayas.

*(**FRED** pulls up a map of India on his laptop.)*

RAJ. That's a pretty big / area –

MRS. KAPOOR. Your Chacha will know.
He's been going to see him because of his cancer.

RAJ. Oh...right. How is he?

MRS. KAPOOR. He's in remission. He says it's been seventy-five percent faith and thirty-five percent diet.

RAJ. That sounds...perfect.

MR. KAPOOR. (Let me speak to him!)

MRS. KAPOOR. Jai stop it. Raju give your Chacha a call. I'll send you his number. Or you know, even better you could Skype or WhatsApp or goober. / He'll be so happy you called him.

MR. KAPOOR. (GOOBER! GOOBER!)

RAJ. That would be great Mom – but do you think you could call him first?

MRS. KAPOOR. I'll call him right now. But don't let this mean I won't hear from you again Raju. If you've still got diarrhea then we have to deal with that –

RAJ. Gotta go.

MRS. KAPOOR. I love you baby boy.

MR. KAPOOR. (BYE!)

*(**RAJ** hangs up.)*

FRED. Should we wait for her to call back?

RAJ. I do not have diarrhea.

7.

*(**RAJ** and **FRED**. They eat their lunch. Green juice. They look hungry.)*

FRED. I have dreams that I'm on a plane and suddenly there's all this turbulence.

RAJ. Then what happens?

FRED. The pilot says that there's a bird caught in the wing. And I'm always like how can one bird cause all this turbulence. And then I look outside and I can see its feathers spewing out of the wing-propeller thing, and the plane is shaking and falling and my stomach is turning and just as I'm about to close down the window I hear this little voice...

And I look around and there it is...the bird sitting next to me.

RAJ. Wearing a seat belt?

FRED. Yeah. Wearing a seat belt.

And the bird is like, "Want to eat my shit?" And I'm like, "No little white pigeon, no thank you I don't want to eat your shit." And the bird is like, "You're in my sky. You think there's no shit in the sky? Like it or not if you're here you will have to eat my shit."

RAJ. Your dreams have a lot of dialogue.

FRED. ...So?

RAJ. Just saying. It's interesting. Mine are more visual.

FRED. Anyway. The next thing I know there's bird shit on my little plastic airplane plate and I've got a fork in my hand and I'm suddenly hungrier than I've ever been before in my life and there I am shoveling bird shit into my mouth and I look around to blame the bird and he's gone.

RAJ. That's extreme, man.

(A moment.)

FRED. It's the same sky.

Wherever you are, it's the same sky.

RAJ. *(Not getting it.)* Yeah...

FRED. But *this* shit, from *this* sky...

RAJ. Yeah?

FRED. This is the shit I want to eat.

RAJ. Yeah...

FRED. American bird shit.

RAJ. Okay, no, I really don't know what you're –

FRED. Do you know what they do to gay men in Singapore Raj?

RAJ. No.

FRED. Two years in prison for holding hands with the person you love.
When I got out I didn't think I was ever going to find a job.

RAJ. Oh god Fred –

FRED. Then I was, like, kind of old and living at home and my mother wasn't speaking to me.
I'd stopped leaving the house.
I'd spend all day looking at the sky.
Then one day I remembered I'd met this guy in Bali on a yoga retreat.
He said he was starting a company inspired by what he'd learned there. And I don't know why but I emailed him.
And he remembered me. The fat Singaporean guy (and I was fat) who couldn't do tree pose.
Next thing I know my papers are stamped and here I am.

RAJ. John did that?

FRED. John did that.
So – I know where my loyalties are.
I'm kind of old fashioned that way.

RAJ. You never said.

FRED. You never asked. I'm not going back Ra–

RAJ. You don't have to.

FRED. No, you don't have to. You can just walk out of here and get a job. Or not get a job. You can go home and your mom will make you Kulfi ice cream and tandoori chicken.

RAJ. That's racist Fred –

FRED. I'm not going back. I'll eat all the bird shit there is to eat.

RAJ. It's going to be okay.

FRED. ...You feel that way?

RAJ. ...

FRED. What?

RAJ. I –

FRED. What?? Whatwhatwhat?

RAJ. I don't really...feel –

(His phone goes.)

It's my uncle –

FRED. Take it!

*(**RAJ** answers.)*

RAJ. Chachaji? Hi, it's Raj! Oh right, you called me, sorry! Uh...can you say that in English –?

FRED. (Don't you speak Hindi?)

RAJ. *(To **FRED.**)* No!

(Into phone.) How are you? I'm so glad you're feeling better. Yeah she told you? Yeah... I'm listening...

8.

*(**RAJ**, **JOAN**, and **FRED**. Joan's office. An aerial view of the Himalayas projected on the wall. **RAJ** holds a laser pointer.)*

RAJ. Haidaram. 120 miles east of Delhi in the Himalayan foothills. Here's where Shri Swami Krishnaram Sitadas Bhagavad Sadhguru Gopal Rajarao but known to his followers as Guruji...

JOAN. (Thank god –)

RAJ. ...Has been living for about five years. Before he arrived in Haidaram, he was living at the foothills of Mount Kailash – which is all the way over here – in the Transhimalayas in Tibet –

FRED. Or China.

RAJ. Or China, depending on whom you talk to. Then five years ago an avalanche forced all the residents out back towards the Indian border. Mount Kailash is hardly habitable. But Haidaram has a population of nearly five thousand so word of him spread pretty quickly.

JOAN. So what is his philosophy?

RAJ. *(Mispronouncing.)* He's reportedly well versed in the Sanskrit texts, the Vedas, the Upanishads, the Mahabharata –

FRED. *(Pronouncing correctly.)* Mahabharata...

RAJ. *(Mispronouncing.)* ...And he apparently also speaks Pearly –

FRED. *(Pronouncing correctly.)* Pali!

RAJ. ...Which is the deadest of the dead languages –

FRED. It's what the Buddha spoke.

RAJ. When he spoke – I mean, I'm not sure he spoke all that much when he was being enlightened –

FRED. Then where did the sutras come from? Aren't they supposed to be his words?

RAJ. Oh yeah –

JOAN. Can we stay on point?

RAJ.	**FRED.**
Sorry.	Sorry.

JOAN. So he's in an ashram? He's accessible?

RAJ. No and kind of.
He lives in a cave.

JOAN. But...your uncle's met him?

RAJ. Well, see, no not exactly.
The cave is at the top of this high hill. My uncle walks this three-mile road cut into the rock. Then there's a footpath marked with chalk which you follow straight up for another mile, until you come to these incredible rock-cut caves...

FRED. Like the Barabar Caves?

RAJ. What?

FRED. From *A Passage to India*...

RAJ. I don't know that book.

FRED. What did you do at Harvard?

RAJ. I spent my time figuring out how to run Fortune 500 companies *Fred.*

FRED. What went wrong *Raj*?

JOAN. Stop it.

(Her breathing gets audibly shallower. **FRED** *and* **RAJ** *don't notice.)*

RAJ. Okay...so my uncle gets there – and there are all these other people there just waiting sitting on the cliff edges. Sometimes there are spontaneous cures and sometimes he'll send you away with a mantra.

JOAN. A what?

RAJ. A prayer – unique to you that you repeat.

JOAN. Like a chant?

RAJ. Yeah – like, you know, sports fans when they all get together and shout things – it's kind of like that but quietly and to yourself and for peace.

JOAN. Thank you for breaking that down.
Does he speak English?

RAJ. My uncle speaks to him in Hindi but he has heard him speak English.

(**JOAN**'*s phone buzzes.)*

JOAN. I'm sorry, this yoga studio keeps hassling me...
I'm turning it off – sorry.

(She does.)

(Her breathing gets louder.)

RAJ. Joan are you okay?

JOAN. Yes...fine.

RAJ. The good news is that my uncle went to see him and made our case for us.
He said we were Americans, that we live in California and we have a great need of him in this moment because our people are suffering.

JOAN. What did he say?

RAJ. He said, "I have known this day would come."

FRED. Holy shit.

RAJ. If you give me the go-ahead he could be here by Friday.

JOAN. Fred!

(**FRED** *goes to pick up the phone.)*

RAJ. He only has one ask –

JOAN. What?

RAJ. He wants us to donate money to several Indian orphanages in the region.

JOAN. How much?

RAJ. Ten million.

JOAN. Rupees?

RAJ. Dollars.

JOAN. Fuck, Raj.

RAJ. I'm sorry I –

JOAN. Call Accounting.
What can we do for your uncle?

RAJ. He's just asked for some Joyon samples for his friends. You can't get really good quality yoga mats in India...

*(**JOAN** picks up the phone and presses the speaker-phone button.)*

JOAN. Nooyi? Nooyi?!

NOOYI. *(From intercom, mid-yawn.)* Yes?

JOAN. Book a one-way flight (we'll figure out the return once he's here.)

FRED. (Seems right.)

NOOYI. Flight, one way...from?

JOAN. ...From...?

FRED. Indira Gandhi Airport –

JOAN. Indira Gandhi Airport to LAX.

NOOYI. Got it! Does he need a cab from the airport?

JOAN. A cab from the airport?
He's been in a cave for fifteen years!

RAJ. He doesn't want to be picked up.

JOAN. What? How's he going to get here?

RAJ. I don't know. But his instructions were that no one comes.

JOAN. I don't want to risk losing him between LAX and here. It's an hour's drive!

RAJ & FRED. Depending on traffic.

NOOYI. So no taxi?

JOAN. Shit you scared me! Nooyi – you have to say something if you're still on the line.

NOOYI. Sorry...
Joan...can I...

JOAN. Not now Nooyi.

NOOYI. I uhm, I, I had a dream last night.

JOAN. What is she talking about?

RAJ.
Dreamtime...

FRED.
Dreamtime...we should listen...

JOAN. (What???)

NOOYI. I was standing in front of a mirror and I was going to put my lipstick on. But every time I twist it to put some on, it crumbled.

JOAN. ...

Is that it?

NOOYI. Uh-huh.

JOAN. Okay. Thank you.

(She hangs up. Her breath catches.)

RAJ. Joan – are you okay?

JOAN. Yes I'm fine...it's just...we're bringing a yogi, a real yogi, all the way here on his own / and what if –

RAJ. Okay. Let's just breathe.

*(**RAJ** and **FRED** hold hands reflexively. **JOAN** slowly joins hands with them.)*

Breathe in through the nose. Out through the mouth with a little sound.

(They breathe in together and hiss out.)

Very good.

In...

Out...

In...

*(**JOAN**'s breath starts to shorten. Her knees start to buckle.)*

Joan.

Joan??

9.

*(**JOAN** and **ROMOLA**.)*

*(**ROMOLA** sits opposite **JOAN**, who is lying on a low bed. **JOAN** wakes and sits bolt upright.)*

JOAN. Am I dead?

ROMOLA. No, you're not dead, you're at the Shakti Elyria Spa and Wellness Institute. And I am Romola.

JOAN. I know who you are! What happened to me?

ROMOLA. You fainted at work. You've been asleep for fifteen hours.

JOAN. *(Checking her watch.)* What? Why didn't they take me to a hospital?

ROMOLA. Do you have a friend Joan?
A real friend?

JOAN. Of course I have...friends.

ROMOLA. Then why was your emergency contact list empty and my card the only card you had in your wallet?

JOAN. I just hadn't had time to fill it up yet! I've been running a company on the brink of –

(Her breathing changes.)

ROMOLA. You can talk to me Joan.

JOAN. Oh no...

ROMOLA. Why not? I am the heart-ear for many Kardashians – I mean, people, who are in the public eye. Celebrities, whose names I can't name, have told me about their childhoods and feelings about their mothers.

JOAN. Listen, Romona –

ROMOLA. Romola.

JOAN. I am not a celebrity. I helped build a coffee company, one that you most certainly have frequented for many a skinny drink. Other people had families and I...I had a brand.

ROMOLA. Why did you leave?

JOAN. ...

ROMOLA. Joan?

JOAN. I couldn't...breathe.
My breath stopped.
So my heart stopped.
And they didn't want me back.

(Her phone goes. She scrambles in her bag for it and answers.)

What do you mean he's here...??? Oh my god... I'm heading right over!

(She hangs up.)

ROMOLA. Oh you can't just leave –

*(**JOAN** looks at **ROMOLA** and then bolts for the exit.)*

You didn't close out with intention!!! NAMASTE YOU BITCH!!!! NAMASTE!!!!

10.

(Joan's office. It's dark. An ill-lit figure sits in a chair. **JOAN**, **RAJ**, *and* **FRED** *enter hurriedly.* **RAJ** *goes to hit the light switch when a soft Indian accent wafts gently through the room.)*

GURUJI. No! No lights!

*(**RAJ** stops.)*

All creation begins in darkness. Let there be darkness.

*(**FRED** takes out his phone.)*

And please – no recording devices.

*(**FRED** replaces his phone in his pocket.)*

Who are we?

What is our purpose?

These questions can be put off until the moment of death.

But why should we wait?

In the Advaita Vedanta we have four states of consciousness.

One we experience in deep sleep.

Two we experience in dreams.

Three we experience when we are awake and,

Four is pure consciousness; *atman*, our true being.

Waking, dreaming, sleeping are ordinary states.

But, to experience *atman*, the inherent bliss of our true nature is very difficult.

In this state who you are and what you are observing becomes one.

You experience unity of all life in its timelessness.

This is called *samadhi.*

To live in *samadhi,* is to experience the joy of *atman* at all times.

To experience *samadhi,* is to know your purpose.

So how can we find it?

How when we are caught up with hankering after objects?
How when we are attached to our bodies as the only source of our identity?
How when we believe our thoughts about ourselves, *are* ourselves?
There is a way to yoke you to *atman*, to your true nature, your purpose.
This.
Is Yoga.
Om Bhur
Bhuva Svaha
Tat savitur varenyam
Bhargo devasya dhimahi
Dhiyo yo nah prachodayat.

(Silence.)

RAJ. Uhm...it seems, uh weird to introduce ourselves now since you've told us our identities are basically not who we are – but I'll do it anyway. So to my right is Fred, Strategic Assistant to Joan and on my left (I think) is our CEO Joan / and I'm Raj – the COO.

GURUJI. Hm.

RAJ. ...Uh / responsible for –

GURUJI. He said you do not have time to waste –

RAJ. That's true –

GURUJI. I want to help you.

RAJ. That's awesome...and please also let me compliment you on your excellent use of the English language –

FRED. (They speak English in India *Raj*.)

RAJ. (I know that FRED!)

FRED. (Then what the hell are you –)

RAJ. (He's been in a freaking cave!)

GURUJI. I want to help you. I want to help you help other Americans to understand this. What is at the core of our unhappiness, our stress, our dysfunction, is a simple misunderstanding of the personality as distinguished from the soul.

JOAN. (He's perfect Raj.)

RAJ. And we are so happy that you are here to help us / do that.

GURUJI. Change takes time but transformation can happen quickly. One thing can turn into another when the pressure is right, the conditions are right –

JOAN. The first thing we'd like to do is to get you to your hotel / for some rest before we –

GURUJI. The answers are all here.

They have always been here.

Sometimes we just have to leave to get them.

*(**RAJ** turns on the light.)*

(A small, clean-shaven white guy sits in Joan's chair.)

*(**RAJ**, **FRED**, and **JOAN** all scream in horror.)*

FRED.	**JOAN.**
Holy shit.	Ohmygod.

RAJ. YOU'RE WHITE MOTHERFUCKER!

GURUJI. Namaste.

ACT II

11.

(Joan's office.)

(Lights up on **RAJ, FRED,** *and* **JOAN** *staring at* **GURUJI.***)*

RAJ. THE FUUUUCK??? / THE FUCK IS THIS?!

FRED. WHAT THE / HELL MAN?

JOAN. WHO IN GOD'S NAME IS THIS?!

FRED. What did you do with our guru???

RAJ. He *is* the guru *Fred*!

FRED. No he's not *Raj*!
Are you?

*(***GURUJI** *nods.)*

JOAN. (Oh my / god, oh my god oh my god...)

FRED. Oh my / god –

RAJ. Oh my / shit!

(He goes over to Joan's desk and grabs the phone.)

I'm calling the police!!

FRED. What are they gonna do?

RAJ. They're gonna arrest him, what do you think?

FRED. For what?

RAJ. For...lying! Wait – no for fraud!
He defrauded us!

*(***GURUJI** *shakes his head quickly.)*

FRED. No he didn't!

RAJ. He made us give millions of dollars to orphana– right / this is not going to work.

FRED. That's not gonna work!

*(**RAJ** slams the phone down and then picks it up again.)*

RAJ. WE'LL SUE YOU! We'll sue the hell out of you for / all the...stones and shit you have in your pockets...fuck!

FRED. For what? What?!

*(**RAJ** slams the phone down again.)*

*(**JOAN** breathes heavily.)*

FRED.	**RAJ.**
Joan???	Joan! Are you okay?

*(The phone rings. **JOAN** hits the speaker button reflexively.)*

JOAN. What is it Nooyi?

NOOYI. *(Through speaker.)* Is everything okay in there?

JOAN. It's fine Nooyi, we're celebrating.

NOOYI. *(Through speaker.)* Yay for the guru! Yay for the –

*(**JOAN** hangs up.)*

RAJ. Is this why you lived in a cave, man? Because you were fooling the good people of India?!

GURUJI. *(Indian accent.)* My...good children...
Let me tell you my story.
My name is...Bernard Brown.
Twenty years ago.
I had that moment.
Many of us have.
I was an English teacher.
At a high school in Santa Monica.
One day I was on the beach looking out on the waves.
I saw them rising and falling, rising and falling.
When I thought –
Who *am* I?

Why *am* I here?
What *are* all these roller blades?
So I left.
I went to India.
I walked for five years until I met my teacher.
I had nothing, I lived on *daana* – donations.
I was searching, searching, searching.
When in the foothills of the Himalayas I found my teacher.
And when he left his body behind on Earth
I followed his example
And meditated for months, then years.
Then...
People started to come.
And I found I knew things.
I could be helpful.
You ask who I am.
I am this.
I am Guruji.

RAJ. Why did you come back?

GURUJI. Because I ran once.
I knew I would have to.
You cannot escape your life – it always finds you.
(To **RAJ.***) Bas-yeh such hai.*

FRED. (What did he say?)

RAJ. (I don't know.)

FRED. (Dude this is like that white woman...)

RAJ. (What white woman?)

FRED. (The one in Seattle who pretended she was black.)

RAJ. (She wasn't pretending – she thinks she really *is* black.)

FRED. (But he thinks he's really Indian!)

GURUJI. *(Indian accent softens a little.)* I may not be who you wanted me to be.

But I have done Sādhanā.
I have done penance.

RAJ.	**FRED.**
Is your accent slipping?	(Heyheyhey...)

GURUJI. ...No.

RAJ.	**FRED.**
Yes it is...	(It's slipping man...)

GURUJI. No it isn't.

RAJ.	**FRED.**
It totally is!	(Totally is...)

What I want to know is –

JOAN. ...Excuse us for a moment!

(She grabs **RAJ** *and* **FRED** *and they huddle. Meanwhile,* **GURUJI** *sits down cross-legged and makes himself comfortable on the floor.)*

Fred?

FRED. Press releases went out this morning –

JOAN. What was the copy?

FRED. That we have India's leading authority in Vedic scriptures / and yogic –

RAJ. We've gotta retract. Shall I call Cassie?

JOAN. Wait – what about the press conference?

FRED. It's Monday.

RAJ. I'm gonna cancel.

JOAN. Wait! We still have the weekend –

RAJ. To do what??

(They look over at **GURUJI** *as a small, equanimous smile spreads across his face.)*

JOAN. You fucked up Raj –

RAJ. (Ohmygod I know that Joan.)

JOAN. But the thing is.
He's perfect.

RAJ & FRED. He's not perfect.

JOAN. But he sounds perfect.

RAJ. But that's / not really –

JOAN. Shhhh.

Let me think.

Just let me think.

(A moment.)

What if we sent him over to hair and makeup?

RAJ. Joan!

JOAN. They could do a beard fitting –

RAJ. That'll never work!

JOAN. What if...we just put some bronzer on him?

RAJ.	**FRED.**
Like, brownface?	Like blackface?
No, no no no no –	Oh right it's brownface –

JOAN. Hollywood does it all the time.

RAJ. And everyone's mad about it!

JOAN. But it always goes away.

RAJ. It's racist.

JOAN. Is it though?

Fred?

FRED. Yes, yes it is Joan.

RAJ. And impractical! What if it rains?

JOAN. It never rains.

GURUJI. I want to help you.

Let me help you.

I have spent fifteen years in the darkness.

So I could be in the light with you.

RAJ. I'm sorry – what is with this accent?

GURUJI. What's with yours?

RAJ. What?

I'm a fucking American!

I'm not pretending not to be!

FRED. Calm down Raj!

RAJ. Don't tell me to be calm.

FRED. This isn't about you –

RAJ. But it is about me – this guy is a fake –
It reflects badly on my culture –

FRED. Your American culture?

RAJ. My Indian culture!

FRED. That you know nothing about?

RAJ. What is your problem?

FRED. Nothing – it's just – nothing.

JOAN. I wish he had a beard...

FRED. Right, not thoughtful.

JOAN. Did your uncle not see him?

RAJ. Motherfucker asked for a robe with a hood!

*(**JOAN**'s breath catches.)*

FRED. You okay?

JOAN. I have to think I have to think I have to think –

RAJ. *(Across to **GURUJI**.)* WHAT THE FUCK?
WHAT THE FUCK DUDE!

FRED. Raj!

JOAN. Why don't we breathe huh?

(They all reach their arms out reflexively toward one another.)

Out.

In.

In.

(She opens her eyes.)

In.

In.

In.

(She drops her arms.)

All right – I've made a decision. Fred, get Marketing to pull some language from our press release. Suggest it's someone young and with sex appeal.

(**FRED** *and* **RAJ** *look over at* **GURUJI**.)

FRED. With all due respect to your taste Joan –

JOAN. Not him.

FRED. Then?

(**JOAN** *looks at* **RAJ**.)

RAJ. OH NO – / OH NO NO NO NO.

JOAN. Raj – yes, yes Raj you got us into this!

RAJ. I know I know and you still can't do this to me! I can't speak Hindi! I don't know anything about Hinduism!

FRED. But – you just said it was "your culture"...

JOAN. He can teach you.

RAJ. That little white guy is not going to TEACH ME about my OWN CULTURE!

FRED. That you know nothing about...

RAJ. It's my culture to not know about!

FRED. That makes no sense.

JOAN. How's your Indian accent?

RAJ. Joan!

JOAN. Bernard can help you – his is wonderful.

RAJ. Why can't Fred do this?

FRED. I'm Chinese.

RAJ. I thought you were part Indian?

FRED. My Chinese side dominates.

JOAN. If we were going with Confucius it would work with Fred.

(**RAJ** *bolts for the door.*)

(**JOAN** *runs in front of him.*)

Raj –

RAJ. You can't / make me do this!

JOAN. It would just be until Monday –

RAJ. Then what?

JOAN. Then we send you to Hawaii for three weeks on the company – and when you come back, nobody notices you've been gone.

RAJ. Tempting and by that I mean not tempting and no. I'm walking.

(He starts to leave. **JOAN** *looks over at* **FRED.***)*

JOAN. If you go, Fred goes too.

*(***FRED** *gasps.)*

RAJ. You can't do that...

JOAN. And with Fred's visa renewal in the mail it would be terrible timing.

*(***FRED** *looks at* **RAJ.***)*

FRED. Raj...

RAJ. Shit Joan.

*(***JOAN** *hits the speaker button.* **NOOYI** *answers.)*

JOAN. Nooyi –

NOOYI. *(Through speaker.)* Yes?

JOAN. Can you take Raj to hair and makeup?

NOOYI. *(Through speaker.)* Sure. Who's it for?

JOAN. Don't worry about that.

Have Accounting draw up new contracts for both him and Fred and have Legal insert a confidentiality clause – oh I want you to sign one too Nooyi.

NOOYI. *(Through speaker.)* A confidentiality clause? Why?

JOAN. Because you're going to be seeing things.

Things you never thought you would see.

NOOYI. *(Through speaker.)* Is someone famous coming by? Ohmygod who?

*(***JOAN** *hangs up.)*

JOAN. How's your practice Raj?

12.

*(**ROMOLA**, **FRED**, and **JOAN**. Romola's yoga studio.)*

*(**ROMOLA** is meditating.)*

ROMOLA. Oh no –

JOAN. *(Eating her pride.)* ...Namaste.

ROMOLA. Don't you fuckin' / namaste me –

JOAN. Romona, I understand –

ROMOLA. It's Romola!

JOAN. Right – look, I owe you an apology.

ROMOLA. Yes you do! I've had to increase my meditation practice because of you!

JOAN. Then I'm hastening your enlightenment!

ROMOLA. You're so full of it!

JOAN. Please – truly, I'm sorry – I just, we've (this is Fred by the way.)

FRED. (Namaste.)

ROMOLA. *(To **FRED**.)* (Hey.)

JOAN. ...Been under a lot of stress lately...

ROMOLA. You're so mean!

JOAN. I'm not mean. I'm just...busy.

ROMOLA. That's what my mom used to say...

(She tears up.)

Oh god – I – I don't know why I'm so emotional lately –

*(**JOAN** gestures to **FRED**.)*

FRED. ...I'm so sorry...about your childhood Romola.
But I have some Jojomon swag here.

*(**ROMOLA** grabs the bag from **FRED**.)*

ROMOLA. But these are Joyon's slow-release lavender-infusion pants...
Oh my god...oh my god.

*(She hugs **FRED** tightly.)*

JOAN. Oh I'm so happy, yay, Pomona we have a bit of an emergency.

ROMOLA. Another yoga emergency?

JOAN. Yes exactly.

We have someone who must perfect his yoga ASAP.

(**ROMOLA** *finally releases* **FRED**.)

ROMOLA. Oh this won't take long!

JOAN. No not him – although – no.

ROMOLA. Where is he?

JOAN. He's uh – he's waiting in the car.

ROMOLA. Oh?

JOAN. He's just...a very special man.

ROMOLA. Is he a celebrity? Because we have a special back entrance / if you need.

JOAN. No, no he's not a celebrity.

He's an Indian guru.

From the ancient town of Haidaram in the high –

FRED. (Low.)

JOAN. Low in the...high Himalayas.

He renounced his life and has been engaged in sitting... down –

FRED. Meditation.

JOAN. Yes sitting down meditation for many years. And now...he wants to understand yoga from a...different perspective.

ROMOLA. You want me to teach an Indian monk yoga?

That is like, *sooo humbling*.

JOAN. I mean, he has a spiritual practice obviously but it's a little bit, you know, esoteric –

ROMOLA. ...What do you mean esoteric?

FRED. She means esoteric.

(He scrolls fast on his phone.)

It means common, familiar, known – oh I'm sorry I looked up antonyms – it means abstruse, arcane...mystic?

ROMOLA. Ohhhh.

JOAN. I think you'll do just fine.

ROMOLA. You don't understand...this is super intense for me because India!
India is the motherland.
If it weren't for the heat and the malaria I'd totally visit.

JOAN. Fred will you get our esteemed guest? He may need your help getting out of the car –

*(**FRED** exits.)*

ROMOLA. Ohmygod – cars must be such a new thing for him.
...I feel my energy shifting already.
It's like a strong force is coming towards me with great speed!

*(**RAJ** enters, holding **FRED**'s hand. He has a large, tangled beehive hairpiece on his head, a fairly decent fake beard, and wears not-quite-fitting orange robes.)*

Oh Jesus.
I mean, Namaste...

(She pauses.)

*(To **JOAN**.)* What should I call him?

JOAN. That's Guru...

*(She looks at **FRED** for help.)*

FRED. Raj.

JOAN. Gururaj.

ROMOLA. Gururaj. It's an honor to meet you.

*(**RAJ** goes to speak –)*

JOAN. He doesn't speak English.

ROMOLA. Oh.

JOAN. He's only been here twenty-four hours.

ROMOLA. Okay – how will we –

JOAN. Fred here knows some Hindo –

FRED. Hindi.

JOAN. He'll translate.

*(**FRED** laughs nervously.)*

FRED. Yeah. But Gururaj mostly likes to speak through gesture.
He thinks we put too much pressure on language for meaning.

ROMOLA. That's awesome! It'll be like silent retreat when everyone's forgotten where the weed is and it's all like –

(She gestures "crazy.")

Woooo!
(Loudly.) GURURAJ PLEASE OVER HERE.

*(**RAJ** flinches at how loud she is. He moves toward her.)*

*(**ROMOLA** takes his hand.)*

(A spark flies.)

What will be the focus of our session together?

JOAN. Well, on Monday we're having a press conference and he's going to have to publicly demonstrate and uh –

FRED. Embody? –

JOAN. Yes, yoga live in front of thousands of fam– I mean, people and he wants to make sure he's fluent in what we do here in our practice.

ROMOLA. Very cool, very cool.
So let's start Gururaj.
Uhm.
LET'S START WITH SOME BASIC POSES.
ARE YOU FAMILIAR WITH SUN SALUTATIONS?

*(**RAJ** looks over at **JOAN**, who looks at **FRED**.)*

*(**FRED** panics, tries to deflect silently, but they stare at him. He makes a quick calculation and speaks some very fake Chinese-inflectioned Hindi.)*

FRED. Burl bashta chai je ye...node SUN SALUTATION?

*(**RAJ** and **JOAN** share a look.)*

ROMOLA. Wow Hindi such a beautiful language...

FRED. Thank you!

*(**ROMOLA** and **RAJ** lock eyes.)*

ROMOLA. We usually begin our yoga practice with setting an intention.
What is his intention?

*(She looks meaningfully at **FRED**.)*

FRED. Ji tooyi ingention?

ROMOLA. Wow "ingention" that totally sounded like "intention."

FRED. English and Hindi are both Indo-Aryan languages.

ROMOLA. I'm getting so much out of this already.
So Gururaj, stand up straight.
Inhale.

*(She breathes in and puts her hand on **RAJ**'s stomach to indicate he should. He likes this.)*

Pull your arms up over your head... *(To **FRED**.)* Can you translate?

FRED. Me? Uh – sure.

*(**ROMOLA** holds **RAJ**'s quads, gently pushing his butt up through the next section. **FRED** translates with his made-up Hindi. He might gesticulate to indicate what he's talking about.)*

ROMOLA. Inhale.

FRED. (Gingale.)

ROMOLA. Come to all fours. –

FRED. Oota tomi allfor –

ROMOLA. Stack your knees –

FRED. Tekkayor dis one –

ROMOLA. Under your hip bones –

FRED. Nunki eta –

ROMOLA. Wrists shoulders –

FRED. Tamar holders –

ROMOLA. Lift your chest –

FRED. Eta ki oota –

ROMOLA. Gaze forwards –

FRED. Eda ke eedar –

ROMOLA. Melt the heart –

FRED. Balo ki tart –

ROMOLA. Lengthen through tailbone –

FRED. Eta ki lagbo tailbon –

ROMOLA. Drop navel –

FRED. Oota nabi –

ROMOLA. Long breath –

FRED. Heeee –

ROMOLA. This is cow position.

FRED. Moooo.

ROMOLA. I think he's getting it! I think he's getting it! Broaden across collarbones.

FRED. Tekkyor dat one ollarhones.

ROMOLA. Lift the navel.

FRED. Ooto da nabi.

ROMOLA. Relax the head.

FRED. Hax da head.

ROMOLA. Lift one leg back –

FRED. Heeft hun heg hack –

ROMOLA. Then the next –

FRED. Den da next –

ROMOLA. Coming into high plank position –

FRED. Jingeng gi hai loo –

ROMOLA. Keep fingers wide –

FRED. Gee ginhers giiide –

ROMOLA. Ground through index finger and thumb.

FRED. Hound hoo da dindex hingerhanhum.

ROMOLA. On your next exhalation –

FRED. Etanaota –

ROMOLA. Untuck feet –

FRED. Tuntuck peet –

ROMOLA. Then slowly lower your knees –

FRED. Putt yor dat one honhor hees –

ROMOLA. Lower hips, belly, arms –
Rise to baby cobra pose –

FRED. (Ssssss...)

ROMOLA. Now press to downward facing dog.
I said downward – oh, right.
Let me...

(She pushes **RAJ**'s *body up to do the pose and slides underneath him.* **JOAN** *gestures to* **FRED** *to stop translating.)*

(Lifting **RAJ**'s *hips with her legs.)* Now lift your hips. They really do love to lift. Lift. Feel your udayana banda –

FRED. *(Unable to help himself.)* Udayana banda –

ROMOLA. Navel lock every time you exhale...

JOAN. Uh Gururaj is indicating he wants you to show him all the poses just like that.

*(***ROMOLA** *scoots out from under* **RAJ**, *lifting him out of his position.)*

ROMOLA. Yoga, as you well know, Gururaj, means union.
Or unity.
With the self.
And with...love.

(She gazes in his eyes.)

Oh Gururaj, you have no idea how nice it is to be in the presence of a man who really listens...

(She unexpectedly takes **RAJ**'s *face in her hands.* **RAJ** *unexpectedly feels something.)*

JOAN. Can you be done by Sunday?

13.

(Night before the press conference. **GURUJI** *is meditating on the floor [and in fact, has been since we last saw him].* **RAJ** *sits in front of him, in his guru robes and hair.)*

RAJ. Hungry?

*(***GURUJI** *shakes his head slowly "no" without opening his eyes.)*

Thirsty?

*(***GURUJI** *shakes his head "no.")*

Didn't you eat in the cave?

*(***GURUJI** *indicates "a little.")*

No mid-afternoon snacks? Granola bars? Truffled almonds?

*(***GURUJI** *is unresponsive.)*

Don't get me wrong, I'm super impressed by this round the clock, no eating, no sleeping, silence thing but in *(He checks his watch.)* twelve hours I'm going to have to know real things about yoga to say in front of real people, so I'd really appreciate it if right about now you could just give me the CliffsNotes...

*(***GURUJI** *is unresponsive.)*

(Leans in.) Look here, we both know I'm the real Hindu because I was born Hindu and that's the only way you can be Hindu so...as ironic as this transaction is – and believe me, the irony is very present for me, I'm willing to concede that an outsider might understand my culture better than me, because that's what the whole idea behind anthropology is, right? (I mean, I don't actually know, I went to Amherst where there was no core so I just did a bunch of – Math and Business apart from the one exception of a vocal production class in my senior year which all the poli-sci and business majors took because we needed to learn

to stop swallowing the ends of our sentences before we went on the job market.)
I wanted to be a banker. Or I wanted to look like a banker.
This is very hard for me man.
Notwithstanding the colonial implications of this scenario, I know that you're a liar and a –
Jesus your feet –
They're like hooves...
My god – is that from all the uh –
The walking?

(**GURUJI** *nods.)*

You walked barefoot?

(**GURUJI** *nods.)*

(A moment of silence.)

Am I learning something?

(**GURUJI** *nods slowly.)*

Right now?

(**GURUJI** *nods.)*

Is it about listening?

(**GURUJI** *nods.)*

(He closes his eyes.)

(**RAJ** *closes his eyes.)*

I just... I can hear my thoughts going round and round like a hamster wheel.
Is that normal?

(**GURUJI** *has no response.)*

Guruji, I have incorporated some meditation into my yoga practice.
But I will reveal now I can't meditate unless my iPhone is no more than six inches away from me.
When I close my eyes I don't see my future.
I see the familiar blue and white lettering of my

Facebook profile.
And the litany of "likes" strewn like lonely leaves
Across the image of my life.

(He stops. A tiny moment of self-reflection.)

(Discovering this.) The *image* of my life
Not my life
Which is spent in a white cube
In front of a screen
That feels like it's alive
That simulates life and living
When in reality I couldn't be further
From the soft touch of a woman's...

*(**GURUJI** opens his eyes.)*

Hands.
A woman's hands you pervert.
I'm frightened...
Of disappointing...
I want to feel...
I want to feel...
Am I learning something?
Is this...is this yoga?

*(**GURUJI** is unresponsive.)*

Dude...are you going to help me with the accent?
Guruji?? Guruji????

14.

(Morning of the press conference. **RAJ** *is asleep on the floor.* **GURUJI** *is in his meditation spot as before.* **FRED** *enters.)*

FRED. Raj?! Raj wake up!

RAJ. Am I dead?

FRED. It's me! Fred!

RAJ. I had a dream that I was on stage. And I was naked. I was holding a microphone but it was unplugged so even though I was saying a lot of things, no one could hear me.

FRED. That's not a dream Raj. That's the plan for today...

RAJ. Oh my god...

FRED. We're just gonna do exactly what we talked about...

RAJ. *(Looking at* **GURUJI**, *in a panic.)* What we talked about?

FRED. *(Not getting it.)* Yeah! You're gonna do the super easy yoga poses Romola taught you and Lauren Lilly Clark Rose is gonna ask you those questions we went over like "What is yoga?"

RAJ. *(Really asking.)* What is yoga?

FRED. Yeah, "What is yoga?"

RAJ. Yeah, what *is* yoga?

FRED. Yeah, what is yoga?

RAJ. No! What is yoga? I don't know what yoga is!

FRED. Wait, but didn't Guruji / talk to you about –

RAJ. Yeah he did!

FRED. So then...?

RAJ. And no he didn't.

It's more complicated / than that –

FRED. Sure, it's complicated but you don't have to go into that

Just give us the CliffsNotes...

(He adds a beard to **RAJ***'s existing beard.)*

RAJ. What are you doing?

FRED. Hair and makeup decided your beard needed a beard, but don't worry, the hair is Indian.

(An elongated floor-length beard falls with a thud on the floor.)

Sorry, sorry. This is just a little bit of (stress.)

RAJ. Of course it's (stress.)

FRED. There would be no (stress) if only you could... (express!)

Have you been able to talk to anyone since all of this...

RAJ. No.

FRED. Why don't you call your mother?

Call her. Get it out of your system

RAJ. They won't understand.

FRED. Call!

RAJ. They'll never understand.

I'm all that matters to them you know!

But, my whole life I've just done what was expected of me.

FRED. At least they're there.

No one's ever stood up for me...

In Singapore I have family

But no home.

And here I'm home

But no family –

Until now.

RAJ. Fred...

FRED. Thank you Raj.

*(**JOAN** enters.)*

JOAN. *(To **FRED.**)* Did you go over the plan?

FRED. I was just / doing that.

JOAN. We have you in the Conference Room. The weave is wonderful.

(Her intercom buzzes. She hits speaker.)

What is it Nooyi?

NOOYI. *(Through intercom.)* Ten minutes and counting.

JOAN. Copy Nooyi.

(A click.)

(To **FRED***.)* Where were you?

FRED. "What is yoga?"

JOAN. Great, truth, authenticity –

FRED. (Jojomon.)

JOAN. Say it with me, truth, authenticity –

FRED. (Jojomon...)

JOAN. Let him say it.

FRED. (Sorry.)

RAJ. Jojomon.

JOAN. Very good.

RAJ. Joan, I can't do this.

FRED & JOAN. Why not?

RAJ. I don't know anything about yoga!

JOAN. That's why we have these...

(She holds up a tiny black object.)

FRED. Micro-mics. Bluetooth, omni-directional so there's no danger of feedback.

Joan and I will be on the left –

JOAN. And Guruji will be on the right. If you run into any trouble, he can help you out.

RAJ. Like, feed me lines?!

JOAN. Yes, exactly, just softly – in your ear, if you need.

RAJ. And you've talked to him about this?

*(***JOAN** *and* **RAJ** *both look over at* **GURUJI** *meditating.)*

JOAN. Yes... I did do that.

RAJ. And he heard you?

JOAN. Uh-huh.

RAJ. Ah...no no no / no no no no –

FRED.	**JOAN.**
Why / not – what's the problem.	Why not, what?

RAJ. What if he doesn't say anything!

JOAN & FRED. Why wouldn't he say anything?

GURUJI. Of course I will.

JOAN. (Thank you so much –)

GURUJI. My pleasure.

FRED. (That's awesome.)

GURUJI. Don't mention it.

JOAN. And if you get stuck, you can give me a little signal...

RAJ. I'm going to be out there alone?

JOAN. Yes.

RAJ. Oh my god Fred!

FRED. *(Pleadingly.)* Raj...please.

*(**RAJ** looks over at **GURUJI**.)*

RAJ. Guruji...?
Will you help me?
Guruji??

GURUJI. I will help you beta.
I am with you at all times.

FRED. Raj?

RAJ. ...
Yeah.
Okay.

JOAN. Okay?

RAJ. Okay.

FRED. Okay!

*(He turns **RAJ** around and fits his mic.)*

*(**JOAN**'s intercom buzzes. She presses speaker.)*

JOAN. What is it Nooyi?

NOOYI. *(Intercom.)* Five minutes and counting.

JOAN. Copy Nooyi!

(A click.)

RAJ. What should my signal be?

JOAN. What signal?

RAJ. You just said to signal you if I needed anything!

JOAN. I said that just to reassure you but okay –

FRED. How about...THANK YOU INDIA?

JOAN.	**RAJ.**
Love it!	No!!!

RAJ. Fred have you ever heard of an Indian thanking India?

FRED. I don't see why not.

RAJ. Because it's a thankless place of poverty and corruption!

FRED. No it's a place of great depth and spiritual beauty just like Alanis Morissette said.

RAJ. She doesn't live there!

FRED. Neither do you!

Oh, one more thing

(small thing)

I think you should make your eyes big.

RAJ. Make my eyes big?

FRED. Yeah – make them big in your head.

(He whips out his phone.)

I saw this awesome YouTube clip of this guru...

RAJ. His eyes are bugging out...

*(**FRED** shows **JOAN**.)*

FRED. I think it's powerful, don't you Joan?

JOAN. I like it.

RAJ. But Guruji doesn't do that with his eyes.

FRED. Guruji's from Santa Monica okay? This guy's in Delhi.

And his eyes are big and it looks good.

*(**RAJ** makes his eyes big. It makes him look stunned.)*

RAJ. Like this?

FRED. Perfect.

RAJ. Do you think there's a special place in hell for people who appropriate their own cultures?

JOAN. If anyone can do it Raj –

FRED. It's you.

(Sorry...were you going to say, "It's you"?)

JOAN. I was.

FRED. (I just...I'm sorry I wanted to say it.)

JOAN. (No problem.)

*(**FRED** dashes over to **GURUJI.**)*

Guruji!

*(**GURUJI** opens his eyes.)*

Here's your microphone. If Raj falters we need you.

*(**GURUJI** nods his head. In that way that can mean yes or no.)*

Keep it simple, introduction, elaboration on the relationship of the Vedas to yoga and yoga to authenticy and authenticity to Jojomon. We're not just a company, we're a –

FRED. Space!

JOAN. We're a –

FRED. Place!

JOAN. We're a –

FRED. Hope!

JOAN. This isn't just about money –

FRED. (It isn't?)

JOAN. Or saving face...

FRED. (Really?)

JOAN. This is about women.

FRED. (Women.)

JOAN. It's about being visible.

FRED. (Visibility.)

JOAN. It's about taking our rightful place in the world no matter what we look like! Or how old we are, or what size we happen to be. It's about stepping forward and being seen for who we are, as valued members of society who work twice as hard, for half as much who can, in a third of the time, get what no man has ever been able to do, done! So we deserve this.

FRED. We really do!

JOAN. Let's breathe!

(Her intercom buzzes. She hits speaker.)

What is it Nooyi?

NOOYI. *(Intercom.)* Live in three Joan.

JOAN. No time to breathe! Go!

*(**FRED** ushers **RAJ** out.)*

NOOYI. *(Intercom.)* Joan, can I / talk to –

JOAN. Not now Nooyi!

*(A click. **JOAN** checks her mic, her breath shortens. She catches **GURUJI** staring at her.)*

Hungry?

*(**GURUJI** shakes his head.)*

Thirsty?

*(**GURUJI** shakes his head.)*

Yoga mat?

*(**GURUJI** smiles at **JOAN**.)*

(He inhales encouragingly.)

(Reluctantly.) Oh...

In

Out

In

In

(A live-streamed video of **RAJ** *comes up on the projection screen. He looks unnaturally tall, maybe because someone's made him stand on a box or elevated platform.)*

JOAN. *(Into her mic.)* Nod if you can hear me Raj.
Raj, nod if you can –

*(***RAJ***, eyes large, nods.)*

(In this moment, with **JOAN** *distracted,* **GURUJI** *slips out of the room.)*

*(***FRED***, miked already, runs back in.)*

FRED. *(Into mic.)* Eyes looking great buddy...

JOAN. *(Off mic.)* Did you tell him to do that?

FRED. *(Off mic.)* I thought you liked it?

JOAN. *(Off mic.)* It looked different in here...

FRED. *(Into mic.)* Huh. It worked on that other guy.

*(***RAJ** *looks confused.)*

(Into his mic.) Oh ho ho you weren't supposed to hear that.
Okay! Let's breathe together!

JOAN. *(Into her mic, unemotionally.)* We already did that!

*(***RAJ** *closes his eyes.* **JOAN***'s intercom goes.)*

(To **NOOYI.***)* What is it Nooyi?

NOOYI.
One minute Joan.
Oh and Lauren's here.

FRED. *(On mic, to* **RAJ.***)*
(In. Out. In.
Now a little snuggle.)

JOAN. *(To* **NOOYI.***)*
Tell her to hold tight, we're still setting up.

FRED. *(On mic, to* **RAJ.***)*
(Very good.)

FRED *(On mic, to* **RAJ.***)* (Goo girl...)

*(***RAJ** *looks confused.)*

JOAN. *(To* **FRED.***)* What are you doing?

NOOYI. *(To* **JOAN.***)* What?

JOAN. *(To* **NOOYI.***)* Not you Nooyi!

FRED. *(To* **JOAN.***)* I don't know what came over me.

(Then, suddenly, a small Skype box pings at the corner of the projection and a woman appears in Jojomon clothing. She looks remarkably like **ROMOLA***, but she's blonde.)*

JOAN.	**FRED.**
Oh shit, she's here.	Shit.

LAUREN LILLY CLARK ROSE. *(Through Skype, projected.)* Hi Joan!
Oh hi...you!

JOAN.	**FRED.**
Give us a moment Lauren, we're just settling Gururaj.	It's Fred.

LAUREN LILLY CLARK ROSE. Where is he I can't...

*(***RAJ***, large-eyed and terrified, pops up in a Skype box.)*

Oh there he is / I see him.

JOAN. *(Into mic.)* She sees you Raj.

LAUREN LILLY CLARK ROSE. He's so cute!

*(***RAJ** *waves awkwardly. He goes to speak and* **JOAN** *cuts in.)*

JOAN. *(Into mic, to* **RAJ.***)* Wait – don't speak Raj.
(Off mic, to **FRED.***)* What is that you have in your hands?

FRED. *(Into mic.)* Raj's weave...

(The intercom.)

JOAN. What is it Nooyi?

NOOYI. Brand ambassadors are in Joan.

JOAN. Thanks Nooyi.
(Off mic.) Why do you have it?

FRED. *(Off mic.)* Why do I have it?
Oh my god I shouldn't have it!
Should I say something?

JOAN. It's too late!

FRED. (It's too late!)

JOAN. *(Into mic.)* Raj. Just remember, keep it simple... Truth, authenticity, / Jojomon –

FRED. *(Into mic.)* Jojomon. Truth, authenticity / Jojomon –

JOAN. *(Into mic.)* ...Jojomon, just as we practiced...and know that if you need help Guruji is right –

*(**FRED** and **JOAN** both turn to look for **GURUJI**.)*

JOAN & FRED. ...There.

(He's gone.)

*(**JOAN** and **FRED** cover their mics...)*

LAUREN LILLY CLARK ROSE. *(Skype.)* Namaste Gururaj! What an honor!

*(**RAJ** nods lamely, maybe a thumbs up?)*

JOAN. *(Covering mic.)* Where is he???

FRED. *(Covering mic.)* He was right HERE!

LAUREN LILLY CLARK ROSE. *(Skype.)* I'm *such* a fan.

JOAN. *(Covering mic.)* Where????

LAUREN LILLY CLARK ROSE. *(Skype.)* How are you doing today?

FRED. *(Covering mic.)* Motherfucker was right here!

*(**RAJ** grins.)*

JOAN. *(Covering mic.)* Fred, find him!

*(**FRED** begins looking hopelessly around the room, under the table, under potted plants, whatever he can find.)*

(Intercom goes.)

What is it Nooyi?

NOOYI.
Mom?

LAUREN LILLY CLARK ROSE. *(To **RAJ**.)*
Who did your makeup?

JOAN. *(To **NOOYI**.)*
What?

(**FRED** *continues to look fruitlessly, in an increasing panic.)*

NOOYI.
I mean, oh god Joan...sorry that's so embarrassing!

LAUREN LILLY CLARK ROSE.
(Looking offstage.)
I love how tan he is.

JOAN. *(Off mic.)*
Not Now Nooyi!

LAUREN LILLY CLARK ROSE.
(Looking offstage.)
Can I get some more bronzer?

(The intercom goes.)

JOAN.
What is it Nooyi?

LAUREN LILLY CLARK ROSE.
(To **RAJ.***)*
Are you ready honey?

NOOYI.
We're uhm live in Boulder Joan?

JOAN. *(Off mic.)*
Fuck!

LAUREN LILLY CLARK ROSE.
(To **RAJ.***)*
You're soooo ready.

FRED. (I can't find him!)

NOOYI. Counting down / Five –

JOAN. Fred!

NOOYI. ...Four...

FRED. He's...

NOOYI. ...Three...

FRED. He's nowhere!

LAUREN LILLY CLARK ROSE. *(To her audience.)* Namaste.

NOOYI. She started!

LAUREN LILLY CLARK ROSE. Dear precious family members...

FRED. *(Off mic.)* Oh my god!

*(**JOAN** and **FRED** continue panickily looking around. **FRED** climbs under Joan's desk.)*

LAUREN LILLY CLARK ROSE. You guys know me as Lauren Lilly Clark Rose...Jojomon's Boulder-based-premiere-brand-ambassador slash life-coach slash life-style consultant...

FRED. *(Off mic.)*
You promised to help him!

JOAN. *(Off mic.)*
I said Guruji would help him!

LAUREN LILLY CLARK ROSE.
...But we're not here to talk about me.
In just one moment, we'll be streaming this special sharing to which press and beloved family are our honored guests to fifty-five countries – live!

FRED. *(Off mic.)* We've got to tell him!

JOAN. *(Off mic.)* YOU TELL HIM.

FRED. *(Off mic.)* NO YOU TELL HIM!

JOAN. *(Off mic.)* NO YOU TELL HIM!

*(**LAUREN LILLY CLARK ROSE** turns her head, and an unidentified hand smoothes down her hair and reapplies some blusher.)*

FRED. *(Into mic.)* Uh Raj, my friend...Guruji is...

*(**RAJ** has temporarily forgotten about his earpieces, he looks like he's received a small shock. His confused face reads "WHAT? HE'S WHAT?!")*

*(**LAUREN LILLY CLARK ROSE** turns back to the camera.)*

LAUREN LILLY CLARK ROSE. And we're worldwide live!

FRED. *(Off mic.)* Oh shit...

LAUREN LILLY CLARK ROSE. Hi! I'm soooo excited to / bring you –

JOAN. *(Off mic.)* What is wrong with her?

LAUREN LILLY CLARK ROSE. From the high / (and low) Himalayas –

FRED. *(Off mic.)* Don't worry, he's got it!
We practiced this!...

LAUREN LILLY CLARK ROSE. The master of pure Vedic yoga.

FRED. Yes Vedic yoga!

LAUREN LILLY CLARK ROSE. Shri Shri Gururaj. Gururaj, Namaste

(The screen splits to show **LAUREN LILLY CLARK ROSE** *and* **RAJ.***)*

JOAN. *(Off mic.)* Oh he looks good!

FRED. *(Off mic.)* He looks great!

LAUREN LILLY CLARK ROSE. And welcome to America.
As someone who has been deep in / meditation –

FRED. So deep in meditation...

LAUREN LILLY CLARK ROSE. ...For many years can you tell us a little bit about what you, as a native of South Asia consider to be yoga?

FRED. *(Into mic.)* YEAH WHAT IS YOGA?!

RAJ. *(Doing his best Indian accent; it's not good but it's heavy.)* Lauren...I can tell you...that yoga / is a...a –

FRED. *(Off mic.)* He knows this!

RAJ. ...Practice from the...ye oldy time...of ancient India.

*(***FRED** *and* **JOAN** *look at each other.)*

LAUREN LILLY CLARK ROSE. Wow...

RAJ. It...is uh the goal / of yoga to achieve...

(He coughs deliberately, touching his earpiece.)

JOAN. *(Into mic.)* (Fuuu / uck.)

*(***RAJ** *starts to say "Fuck," but then stops just in time.)*

RAJ. Fffffour...four uh...

*(**FRED** rifles madly through his notes.)*

FRED. *(Into mic.)* Noble truths? Fuck that's Buddhism! SHIT.

*(**RAJ** hears the end of **FRED**'s "shit.")*

RAJ. Shit... Pur-shit-ttass.

*(**LAUREN** looks confused.)*

Pur-shaatt-ass? Puru-shaaaaathass!

LAUREN LILLY CLARK ROSE. Gosh so embarassing. I've always said *(Pronouncing it correctly.)* Purusharthas.

*(**RAJ** touches his hair / earpiece purposefully.)*

RAJ. That uh...

(He looks long into the camera in desperation.)

(Hesitantly.) Thank you... India.

*(**JOAN** and **FRED** stare at each other.)*

(With greater conviction.) India! Thank you!

LAUREN LILLY CLARK ROSE. Oh...

FRED. *(Off mic.)* Joan...

RAJ. INDIA? Thank YOU.

FRED. *(Off mic.)* Joan?

RAJ. India? / India??

JOAN. *(Off mic.)* Let me think!

RAJ. India thank you?!

FRED. *(Off mic.)* Joan!

RAJ. India???

FRED. *(Off mic.)* He's not stopping!

JOAN. *(Off mic.)* Say something!

RAJ. YOUUU. INDIA. THANK.

LAUREN LILLY CLARK ROSE. We're not grateful enough to India it's true...

JOAN. *(Off mic.)* Fred!

FRED. *(Off mic.)* I can't!

RAJ. *(Like "fuck you.")* THANK YOU INDIAAAAA!!!!

JOAN. *(Into mic.)* Okay. Raj...listen to me, okay?
Guruji isn't here.
Okay?
Raj...
I'm really sorry.
He's gone.
You're on your own.

*(**RAJ** stares at the camera, the truth of his situation dawning on him. He looks down at his empty folder; his bad Indian accent oscillates dangerously.)*

LAUREN LILLY CLARK ROSE. So, for our million viewers Gururaj...let's cut through right to the chase.
What is yoga?

JOAN. *(Into mic.)*	**FRED.** *(Into mic.)*
You can do this Raj...	Come on buddy...

RAJ. Uh...so...there are four uh...types of...things.
So how to balance...all them things?
Truth...

JOAN.	**FRED.**
Yes, truth...	Yes...

RAJ. Authenticity...

FRED.	**JOAN.**
Authenticity	Good, authenticity...

RAJ. More truth...

FRED.	**JOAN.**
More truth.	More truth?

RAJ. And...more authenticity...

FRED.	**JOAN.**
No more authenticity.	Nope!

LAUREN LILLY CLARK ROSE. Wow...

RAJ. The thing about truth Lauren...

LAUREN LILLY CLARK ROSE. Yes???

RAJ. It's very authentic.
And the thing about authenticity is that it's very Truth. So these are...very...complicated / uh –

LAUREN. So complicated...

RAJ. – Things, but in my country of...

LAUREN.	**FRED.** *(Into mic.)*	**JOAN.** *(Into mic.)*
India?	INDIA!	INDIA!

RAJ. Yes... India...
...We have this ancient practice in our bones as naturally as the sun rises in the, the –

LAUREN.	**JOAN.** *(Into mic.)*	**FRED.** *(Into mic.)*
East!	East!	East!

*(**RAJ** pauses suddenly. Trapped, he closes his eyes.)*

(With nowhere to go, he inhales deeply; for the first time, he goes within. Everything stills.)

LAUREN LILLY CLARK ROSE. Gururaj?

*(**RAJ** opens his eyes, his defenses are down, he looks directly and openly into the camera. With nowhere to go, he surrenders, dropping the accent, discovering his thoughts as he goes along.)*

RAJ. Brothers and Sisters of America... I don't know very much but I do know this...the answers can't be outside us.

JOAN. *(Into mic.)*	**FRED.** *(Into mic.)*
YES RAJ!	BRING IT RAJ!

RAJ. They have to be within.

JOAN.	**FRED.**
Yes it's within!	WITHIN!

RAJ. We've got to take correct action...

FRED. ACTION!

RAJ. Make ethical / choices –

FRED.	**JOAN.**
ETHICS!	ETHICS YEAH!

RAJ. ...That is all we can do / as human beings...and so...

FRED.	**JOAN.**
He's got it!	He's done it Fred!

*(**RAJ** reaches into his hair and turns off his earpiece.)*

What's happening?	What's he doing?

RAJ. So...there can be just one small secret to eternal bliss.

LAUREN LILLY CLARK ROSE. Tell me Gururaj!

*(**RAJ** pauses dramatically.)*

RAJ. Stop. Buying. Things.

JOAN.	**FRED.**
No...	No...

RAJ. You don't need yoga mats!

JOAN. He's going rogue!

FRED. *(Into mic.)* Abort Raj! Abort!

RAJ. You don't need expensive pants!

FRED. *(Into mic.)* Raj?! Do you read me?!

LAUREN. *(Murmuring.)* But they're so comfortable...

JOAN. *(Off mic.)* Get him out of there...

FRED. *(Off mic.)* He can't hear me!

RAJ. *(Talking fast.)* Every time you buy, you stop / listening to YOU.

JOAN. ...We have to get him off.

RAJ. You block the channel.

JOAN. Now! Go!

*(**FRED** runs out.)*

RAJ. And if you cannot hear... / you cannot feel

JOAN. ...Call Operations!

RAJ. ...And if you cannot feel...it is like you are going through life in a dream.

LAUREN LILLY CLARK ROSE. *(Choked up.)* But Jojomon has been like a family to me Gururaj...

JOAN. Nooyi!

RAJ. Your family will love you with or without your things Lauren Lilly Clark Rose...

LAUREN LILLY CLARK ROSE. I love how you say my name...

JOAN. Someone pull the plug!

(The picture goes to black. Both **LAUREN** *and* **RAJ** *have gone.)*

*(***FRED** *runs back in with some stray wires in his hands.* **JOAN** *rips her mic off, breathing heavily.)*

FRED. I did it!

JOAN. Is a little loyalty too much to ask for?!

FRED. Me?? I am loyal! My mother says it's my only good trait!

JOAN. Not you, Raj!

FRED. Raj doesn't need this job Joan!

JOAN. *(Losing it.)* You're both assholes! Do you know what my life has been? Can't seem too competent because then I'm a bitch, can't seem too submissive because then I'm weak! Do you know the shit I've had to eat?

FRED. Actually, yes!

JOAN. Do you know why?

FRED. Actually, no!

JOAN. Because women don't get second chances Fred.

(She holds her head in her hands. Against her better judgment and all the will in the world, she begins to cry. **FRED** *involuntarily reaches for her and hugs her.)*

FRED. Oh Joan...

*(***RAJ** *enters, still in his robe and beard.)*

*(***JOAN** *and* **FRED** *turn to see him.)*

JOAN. Judas!
You put us all on the line!

RAJ. I know –

JOAN. Not just me – and your friend here!

RAJ. (Hey Fred.)

FRED. (Hey Raj.)

JOAN. There are eleven thousand other people who work here...

(A sudden, small explosion from **FRED**'s *phone.)*

*(***FRED** *checks it.)*

FRED. Jesus...

*(***JOAN**'s *breath catches in her throat.)*

Joan...

JOAN. Not now / Fred...

FRED. No.

JOAN. I just can't –

(Her breath gets tighter and tighter in her throat.)

FRED. Listen we're...

JOAN. I told you no!

(Her knees begin to buckle. **FRED** *catches her.)*

FRED. Our shares are up over sixty-five percent!

JOAN. Am I dead?

FRED. Our website's crashing from online sales!

JOAN. I don't understand...

FRED. ...Social media's all over it, #gurusaysdontbuy.
They bought it Joan.

JOAN. Our clothes?

FRED. The story.

JOAN. Raj?
But...he was horrible.

FRED. I know!

JOAN. But…why?

RAJ. Because I told the truth.

(Intercom buzzes.)

JOAN. What is it Nooyi?

NOOYI. *(Intercom.)* Romona is here for Gururaj…

ROMOLA. (It's ROMOLA!)

(She barges in.)

RAJ. Romola!

NOOYI. *(Intercom.)* She's inside.

JOAN. Yes we know, we can see her.

ROMOLA. Namaste Gururaj…

I'm sorry for coming back here!

I just wanted to tell you.

You were so…awesome out there Gururaj…

I closed my eyes and I could hear your voice and smell the lavender in my pants…and it was all…

RAJ.	**ROMOLA.**
Like samadhi…	Like samadhi…

ROMOLA. Bliss.

And your English has improved soo much, it's sooo inspiring…

(She goes up to **RAJ.***)*

Take me with you Gururaj…

RAJ. Yes…

Where?

ROMOLA. To the motherland.

FRED.	**JOAN.**
Delaware?	Delaware?

ROMOLA. India.

We could go backpacking!

RAJ. We will do it…together.

ROMOLA. Whaaaaat? Really?

(She takes **RAJ***'s face in her hands. They kiss.)*

RAJ. Will you...give us one moment Romola?

ROMOLA. *(To* **RAJ.***)* Namaste.

RAJ. *(To* **ROMOLA.***)* Namaste.

ROMOLA. *(To* **FRED.***)* Namaste.

FRED. *(To* **ROMOLA.***)* Namaste.

ROMOLA. *(To* **JOAN.***)* Namaste

JOAN. *(To* **ROMOLA.***)* Now go away.

*(***ROMOLA** *bows deeply. She exits.)*

RAJ. I...I don't expect you to understand Joan...
But out there when I was alone...(maybe it was the fear) but my mind went totally quiet. And then...this voice spoke...and it didn't feel like mine but it came through me and it was connected to my heart and for the first time in my life...I could feel.
We can't afford to numb our pain anymore.
Not even with yoga.

(He goes to leave.)

JOAN. Where do you think you're going?

RAJ. Just...outside.

JOAN. You're coming back?

RAJ. Totally.
I mean.
(To **FRED.***)* We'll figure this out Fred.
Peace.

(He exits.)

(A moment. **FRED** *summons his courage.)*

JOAN. Fred, I need to call a / board meeting –

FRED. Joan –

JOAN. ...And I need the percentages for the / full trading day today.

FRED. Joan.

JOAN. What?

FRED. I have two words for you.

JOAN. Yes?

FRED. Green card.

JOAN. Fred.

FRED. Say it.

JOAN. No!

FRED. Green card.

JOAN. No way!

FRED. greencardgreencardGREENCARD!

JOAN. (Shit Fred.)
Green card.

FRED. Thank you.
Now one more.
Sabbatical.

JOAN. Absolutely not.

FRED. Fine, two weeks paid leave.
I want to go home.

JOAN. What's at home?

FRED. My mother.
And someone else who I haven't seen in a long time.
I have a question for him.
I didn't ask the last time.
Because I was too scared.
Of all the shit in the sky.
I can't live in fear.
I can't do it.

(He exits.)

*(**JOAN** looks after him.)*

(Alone.)

(She looks around, lost. Her breath starts to shorten.)

(She looks over at Guruji's meditation spot.)

(She goes over to it and sits.)

JOAN. *(To herself.)* I did it.

I won.

But, I...I'm –

(Lights shift. **GURUJI** *appears.)*

I'm all alone.

But that's...

We're all, all alone.

GURUJI. You are not alone.

You are never alone.

JOAN. Am I asleep?

GURUJI. You're just waking up.

JOAN. I...have this dream. There are ants climbing all over my face. They're crawling all over me. And I look down and I realize, every single ant has a face, every single one, has a name...and I can't step on them anymore, I can't...do it so I'm standing there covered in ants, blackened from head to foot and I'm itching all over and yet, I can't move.

GURUJI. That's compassion.

JOAN. For the ants?

GURUJI. If everyone felt that kind of respect for the ant it would be a different world.

JOAN. I just wanted to matter...

To do something that matters...

GURUJI. You do not have to do something to matter.

You are not a human doing.

You are a human being.

(He drops his accent. A moment of honesty.)

When you connect to your true self.

You will know who you are.

You will know how to act.

This. Is Yoga.

Listen.

*(***JOAN*** sits a moment.)*

(She listens. She breathes.)

(In.)

(Out.)

(In.)

(Out.)

(In...)

(Out.)

(For the first time in the play, her mind stills.)

(As she breathes, the world of her office falls away around her...and she sees the universe bursting with light. Samadhi.)

(She gasps in wonder.)

(Then, her cell phone rings.)

(Blackout.)

End of Play